VISUAL SCIENCE

TELECOMMUNICATIONS

John Stevenson

Macdonald Educational

Editor Daphne Butler
Editorial assistant Barbara Tombs
Design Richard Garratt
Consultant Alan Cooper
Picture Research Caroline Mitchell
Production Susan Mead

A MACDONALD BOOK

© Macdonald & Co (Publishers) Ltd

First published in Great Britain in 1984
by Macdonald & Co (Publishers) Ltd
London & Sydney

A member of BPCC plc

ISBN 0 356 07115 4

Printed and bound in Belgium by
Henri Proost, Turnhout, Belgium

Macdonald & Co (Publishers) Ltd
Maxwell House
74 Worship Street
London EC2A 2EN

Cover: A microwave link station in Scotland using tropospheric scattering for communicating with offshore platforms in the North Sea gas and oil fields.

Right: Light patterns in the ends of optical fibres.

21117955V

TS

21117955V

TS

Contents

Sharing information

Imagine what it would be like to be stranded at home with no radio, telephone or television. Imagine not being able to send or receive letters, newspapers or books. You would feel very isolated. People living 200 years ago would not have understood your feelings – that was how they lived.

Today we are used to watching events as they happen. It may be the final of the World Cup or the opening ceremony of the Olympic Games. Personal news also travels very quickly. Relatives can be told of the arrival of a new-born baby by telephone within minutes of the birth, even if they happen to live on the other side of the world.

This tremendous speed and ease of communication is really quite new. In 1805 news of the Battle of Trafalgar took 16 days to reach London.

For many centuries the fastest way of sending a message was to use a man on horseback. Letters were very expensive to send – or rather to receive, as it was the receiver who paid! Anyway, few people could read or write. So most people only kept in touch with those they could personally visit.

Better roads and the coming of the railways led to more people travelling further. People in business and politicians have always wanted up to date information, especially if they could get it before their rivals.

This is where telecommunications come in. Telecommunications are all about sharing information over some distance. 'Tele' is a Greek word meaning 'far'. This, together with another Greek word 'graphein' meaning 'to write', gives us the word 'telegraph'. A telegraph is a device which can send a coded message a long way. The word was first used to describe Chappe's optical telegraph in 1794. His system was rather like a mechanical semaphore.

Inventions we take for granted today were often greeted with little enthusiasm. The invention of the telephone was given a luke-warm reception in Europe. People said that it was very interesting but too expensive. It was seen as an intrusion on privacy. Anyway, there were plenty of servants to carry messages.

Governments, too, sometimes seemed reluctant to accept new technology. In 1816 Sir Francis Ronalds presented to the British Admiralty his ideas for an electrical telegraph to replace their mechanical semaphore system. But they refused to accept the new method,

saying there was no future in it. Forty years later the electric telegraph was well established.

However, even governments realise the value of telecommunications in times of war. The First World War gave the development of radio a big boost. In the Second, radar was rapidly turned into an extremely effective aid to defence against enemy aircraft, ships and submarines.

When the telephone was invented, a hundred years ago, it was the first communications device which did not require any special skills to use it. Now long-distance cables and satellites provide a cheap and efficient means of communication all over the world.

Broadcasting has changed dramatically since it was first introduced just a

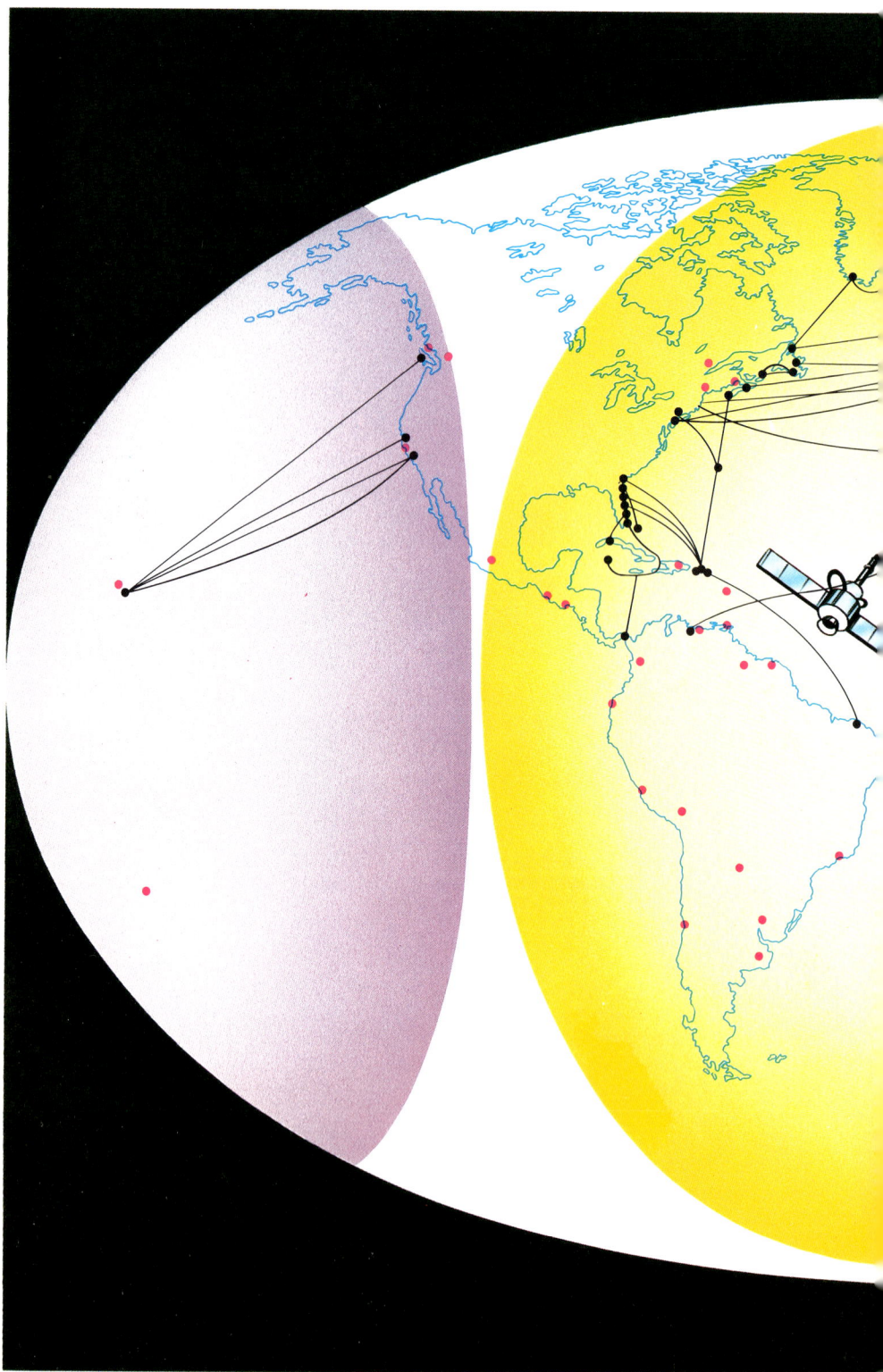

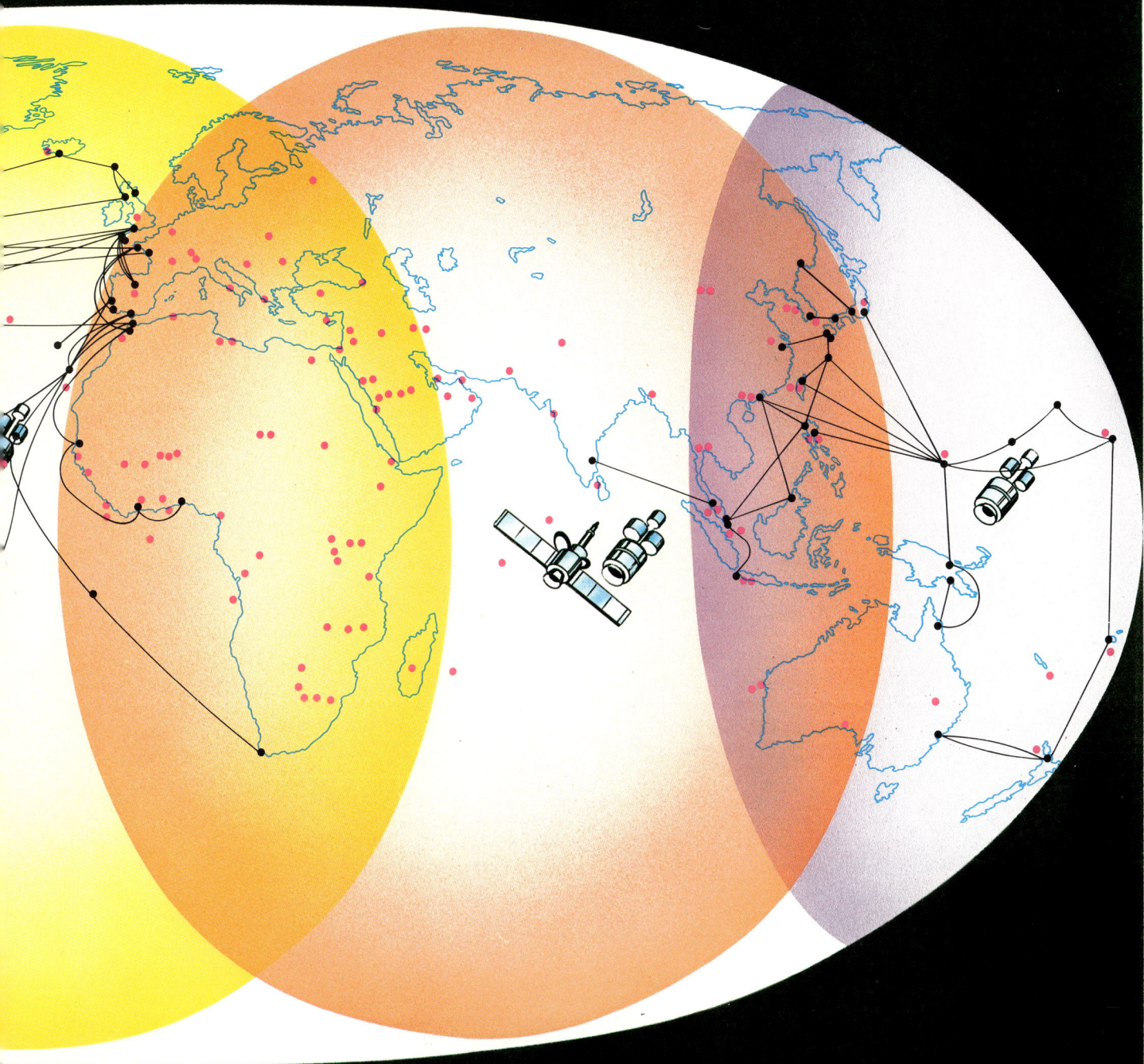

little over 60 years ago. Amateur radio has flourished and today CB (Citizens' Band) radio has quickly caught the public imagination.

Telecommunications really began when little pulses of electricity were sent down metal wires, about 150 years ago. Over the last 20 years the silicon chip has revolutionized telecommunications. The speed, size and cheapness of the chip has made possible many systems, such as electronic telephone exchanges. Now a second major change may be taking place. It is based on another form of silicon – glass. Instead of using pulses of electricity, flashes of light are used. And the metal wires are replaced by thin strands of glass. Over the next few years we shall see to what extent optical fibres replace exisiting technologies.

Above: This map shows parts of the 'biggest machine' in the world. Over 150 countries co-operate to make international communications possible. Modern telecommunication routes follow long-established trade routes and are concentrated in approximately one-third of the world. On the map black lines are telephone cables and black dots the cable stations. The red dots are Earth satellite receiving stations.

Early days

Early people lived in a dangerous world. Survival was difficult, and life was short. Working together increased the chances of survival. So people lived in groups, or communities. The members of a community share and co-operate together. Communication is the means of doing this. Also, once people could communicate, they could pass on their experience and knowledge to others.

Through the development of speech, it became possible to communicate ideas and emotions, as well as facts. Drawing and painting were also developed and used for communication.

Speech is not much good for long distances. Shouting is a simple way of communicating. By spacing people out, within shouting distance of each other, it is possible for a message to be sent quickly from one place to another. But you need a lot of people with very powerful voices, and good ears.

Messages using drums can be relayed over great distances. A drum can be heard up to 10 km away, and the message passed on from one drummer to another. In a similar way a message can also be relayed using smoke signals, fire or flags.

A reliable way of sending a message was to take it yourself – or to pay some-one to take it for you. Today's marathon originates from the Greek messengers who ran long distances.

Writing

When people needed to keep records they had to devise a means of writing. The first written signs were the Sumerian pictographs from 3000 BC. They were really little pictures of objects. Gradually these developed into ideographs which could also represent ideas. Then the symbols began to stand for sounds. This drastically reduced the number of symbols required. From these early symbols our modern alphabet evolved.

In the Middle Ages few people could read or write. Every book had to be copied by hand, usually by monks. They started by making the paper and finished by binding the beautifully illustrated pages together. As a result, books were very rare and expensive.

Printing

In Asia and China printing using wooden blocks had probably existed since the 5th century AD. The blocks for each page of a book took a long time to carve. In the 15th century, Johannes Gutenberg of Germany became famous for bringing together various ideas and inventing a system of printing that was to have a great effect on history. Using this system, books could be made quickly and at a relatively low cost. This made them available to more people, and new ideas could spread rapidly.

Above: Nelson's flagship *Victory* during the Napoleonic Wars. Ships used flags to send messages and battle orders. Special military codes prevented the messages being understood by the enemy.

Below: Once proper roads were built it was possible to send mail by coach. Two hundred years ago when the mail coach service started it took three days and three nights to travel from London to Edinburgh.

Newspapers

In the 17th century newspapers began to appear regularly. They tended to be very critical of the government. A heavy tax was put on them to try and stop their distribution but this was unsuccessful. Today, newspapers are still one of the most effective means of communicating news and opinions.

Mail

For centuries it has been possible to send a message by post. It was the person who received the letter who had to pay. The charges were so high that only the wealthy could afford to use the service. Not until the introduction of the penny-post in 1840 could most people in England afford to send a letter.

Optical telegraph

It was the invention of the telescope that made faster communication over long distances possible. A brilliant French engineer, Claude Chappe, started to build a communications system for the

military to use in 1790.

Chappe built a series of towers about 20 km apart. On the top of each tower was a pair of wooden arms. Each position of the arms stood for a letter of the alphabet. Telescopes were used to see what letter the tower along the line was sending. This was then sent on. Messages reached their destination more quickly than ever before. One message took three minutes to travel 800 km.

Above: Egyptian writing, called hieroglyphics, was a mixture of ideographs and phonetics. A symbol could represent either an idea or a sound. People wrote using pen and ink, on papyrus, a kind of paper made from reeds.

Above left: One of the dramatic cave paintings from Lascaux in south-west France. It was painted during the Stone Age, over 15,000 years ago.

Right: In 1860 the Western Pony Express provided a regular service between New York and San Francisco (4,000 km). It went out of business in 1862 when the transcontinental telegraph was completed.

Telegraphs and railways

Above: Galvani, experimenting on the legs of dead frogs noticed that sometimes they twitched. Volta, trying to explain this behaviour, came upon the ideas leading to his invention of the battery.

Below: In 1774 Georges Lesage built one of the first electrostatic telegraphs. If a wire touches the electrostatic machine an electric shock travels down the wire and moves an indicator at the other end.

If you rub a plastic comb on your sleeve you can make it pick up small pieces of paper. Sometimes you can hear a crackling noise as you take off a piece of clothing made from synthetic material. This is due to static electricity. Several inventors suggested using static electricity to make an electric telegraph.

Static electricity is made by friction – one material rubbing against another. Over two hundred years ago scientists had invented machines to make static electricity. These machines were very popular and entertaining. Showmen could give people shocks and explode gunpowder with the sparks!

Electricity was found to travel through metal wires extremely quickly. As it travels so quickly several people thought electricity might be useful as well as fun to play with. Don Francisco Salva of Barcelona suggested an electric telegraph in which the operators at the receiving end got electric shocks!

The first telegraphs

In 1820, twenty years after Volta invented the battery, Hans C. Oersted showed that electricity and magnetism were connected. He passed an electric current through a wire which made a nearby compass needle move. A Russian diplomat, Baron Schilling was one of several inventors who used this effect as the basis of a new kind of telegraph.

Emperor Nicholás I of Russia commissioned a Schilling telegraph to link St Petersburg and the imperial palace at Peterhof.

By this time the fastest means of travelling, or sending a message, was by train. An electric telegraph which could send a message much faster than a train could clearly be used to improve the safety of the railways. In England, Cooke and Wheatstone demonstrated their telegraph to the directors of a railway company in 1837. The Great Western Railway was the first to use one of Cooke and Wheatstone's telegraphs. These telegraphs were used to indicate when it was safe for a train to proceed. The illustration below shows what one looked like. But development was slow. The railways were slow to extend the system, probably because of cost.

International co-operation

Telegraph wires were run alongside railway lines at first, and then roads. But, to begin with, they stopped at the borders between countries. This meant that at the frontier between France and Germany, for example, there had to be two people. At the end of the line from Paris,

the Frenchman would write the message down on a piece of paper and push it across the table to his German colleague. He then had to translate it into German and send it on its way. This complicated procedure delayed the messages considerably.

Soon nations began to co-operate and to agree ways of sending telegrams from one country to another. In 1852 it was agreed that telegraph wires could be constructed across borders. The success of telegraphy was not just due to scientists and engineers but also to international co-operation.

Newspapers were among the first users of the telegraph and helped the network of telegraph lines to expand. Obviously the newspaper with the most up to date news was going to sell more copies than its competitors.

By the middle of the 19th century news could travel between the major cities of Europe in a few minutes instead of days and weeks. Julius Reuter was one of the most imaginative users of the telegraph. He made his fortune by collecting and distributing news. Today, Reuters is a major agency for collecting and distributing news worldwide.

Below: Cooke and Wheatstone's telegraphs worked by passing electric currents down wires which deflected magnetic needles at the receiving end.

Two wires were used, and two magnetic needles. A code had to be used too, as there were many more letters of the alphabet than positions of the needles. For instance, one leftwards flick of the left needle stood for the letter 'e'.

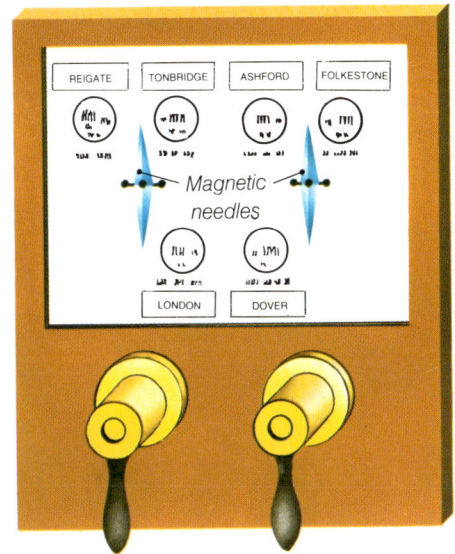

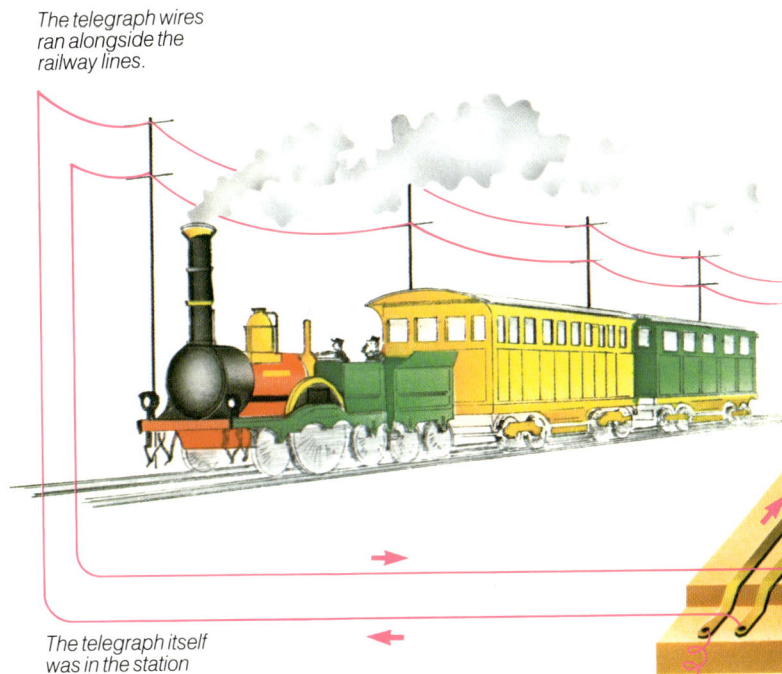

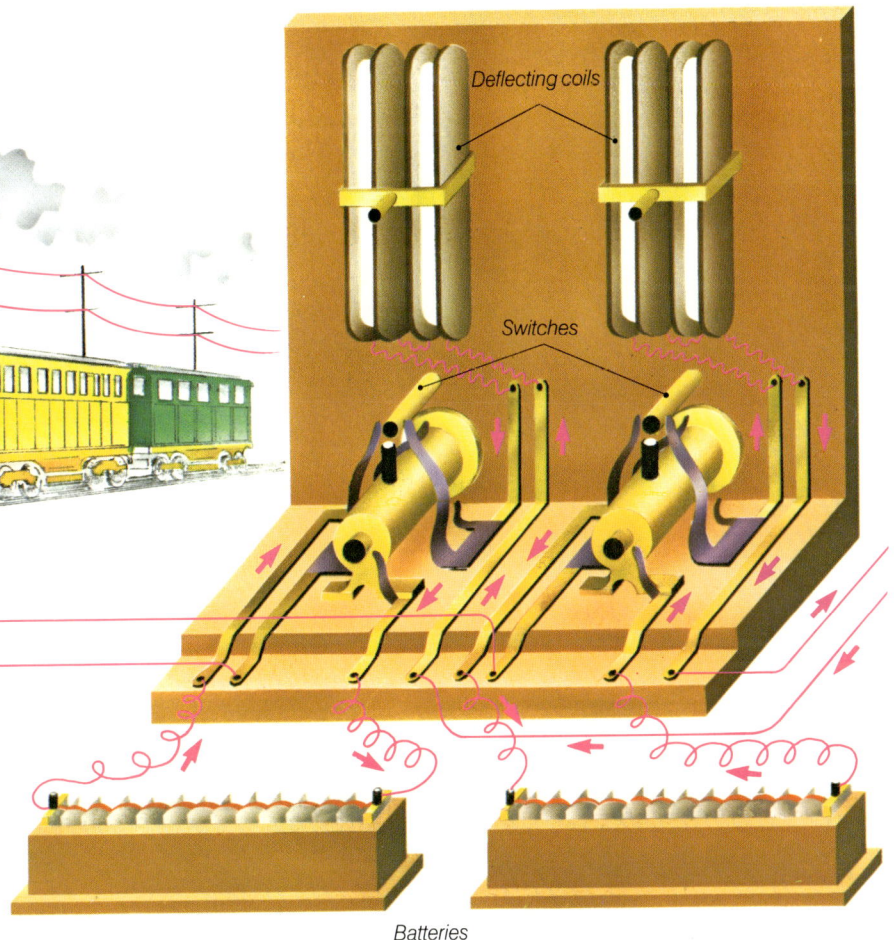

REIGATE TONBRIDGE ASHFORD FOLKESTONE

Magnetic needles

LONDON DOVER

The telegraph wires ran alongside the railway lines.

The telegraph itself was in the station

Deflecting coils

Switches

Batteries

9

Telegraphy expands

Above: The Central Telegraph Office in Paris about 1860 showing the many operators at work.

Below: Morse's Telegraph, 1845, made a permanent record on a piece of paper of the message received.

It was a professor of art, a distinguished painter, who introduced the telegraph to America. We remember him because he also invented a code which became world famous and is still used today. His name was Samuel Morse. In 1832 he went on a tour of Europe to study art. On the return voyage another passenger showed him the principles of electromagnetism on which the electric telegraph is based. Morse was so intrigued that he immediately tried to build a practical telegraph. He worked out that it was possible to send a message electrically along a wire and record it permanently on paper as a series of dots and dashes.

On 1 January 1845 a telegraph line was opened between Baltimore and Washington using Morse's ideas. Many European countries also based their telegraph systems on his ideas. In England the telegraph companies were privately owned and this tended to hinder progress. People complained of the high charges and poor service. Eventually in 1868 the telegraph companies were nationalized and were run by the state.

In spite of these initial problems, telegraphy expanded rapidly. The first conference of the International Telegraph Union was held in 1865 and the 21 countries involved had half a million kilometres of telegraph lines between them.

As the use of the telegraph increased one disadvantage of the Morse equipment was soon noticed. Before it could be sent, the message had to be converted into dots and dashes. Afterwards, someone in the receiving telegraph office had to convert it back again and write the telegram onto a piece of paper. Scientists and engineers began to look for ways of sending messages along telegraph lines which did not involve the operators converting messages into code and back again.

David Hughes, a professor of music at New York University, devised a way to send a message directly. The sender had a keyboard in front of him, rather like that of a piano, but with letters on it. He just typed the message. At the receiving end the message was printed onto a strip of paper. Naturally the mechanics were very complicated but it doubled the speed at which messages could be sent over the wires and was also much more convenient.

Multiplexing
In 1853, Dr Wilhelm Gintl of Vienna

devised a way of sending a message in both directions at once along the same telegraph wire. It doubled the number of messages that could be sent. The technical word for this is a 'duplex' operation. The invention was obviously of great benefit to the telegraph companies, as it doubled the amount of money they could make from a single line. Other inventors began to look for ways of sending more than two messages along a wire at the same time.

In 1874, Thomas Edison devised and patented a method of sending four messages along a wire, two in each direction. Emile Baudot, of the French Telegraph Service, was another. He developed the first practical system for several people to use the same line at the same time. This is called Time Division Multiplexing (TDM).

Engineers were not content with sending just words as quickly as possible through wires. Telegraphs were devised which could send pictures or photographs. Now the telegraph system has grown into a large international system called telex. Most large businesses have their own telex teleprinter which can send and receive printed messages, to and from anyone in the system.

Right: Many different codes are used to send messages. Here, the international call for help, SOS, is being sent in five different ways. Some of the codes illustrated here are familiar and in use today. Others, such as the code for the early shutter telegraph and the code for Cooke and Wheatstone's 5-needle telegraph are now obsolete.

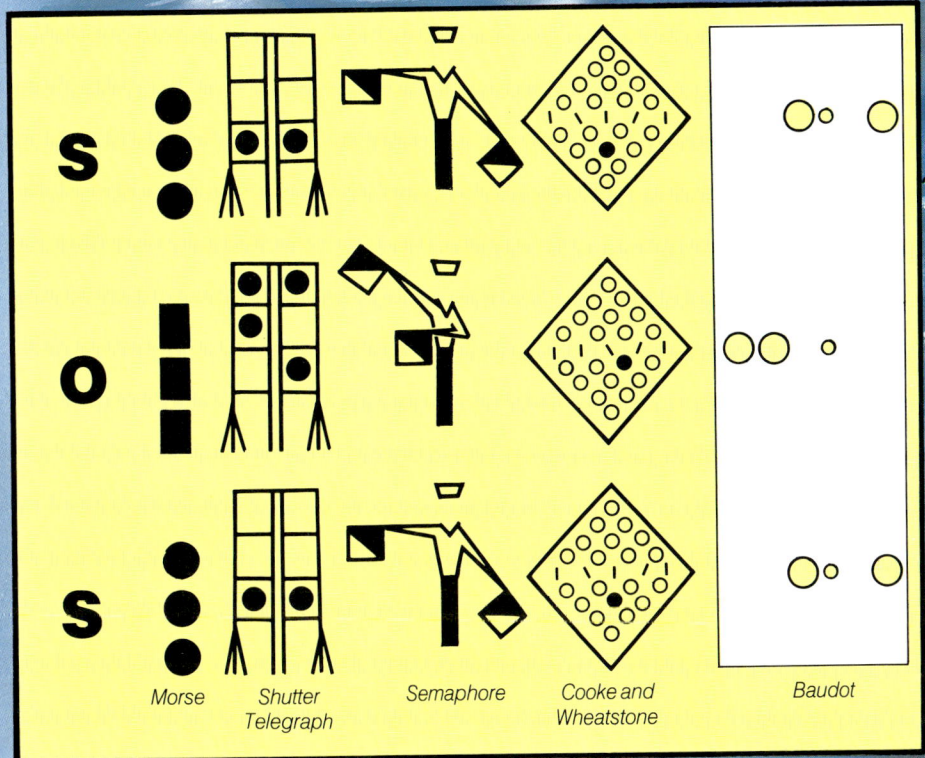

| Morse | Shutter Telegraph | Semaphore | Cooke and Wheatstone | Baudot |

Cables under the sea

Left: Modern cable laying and repair ships have lots of specialized equipment on board. They have the latest aids for navigation and communication. Helicopters can land on them and the amenities for the crew are also very good.

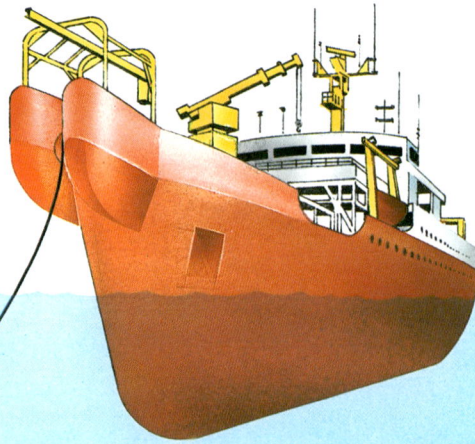

At first telegraph wires were hung from poles alongside railway lines, canals and roads. In some places the wires were laid underground in special ducts. By 1850 the major cities of Europe were linked together. But there was still a big barrier for the telegraph – the sea. The large network in England was still not connected to that of Europe.

The European link
In 1843 it was discovered that gutta percha, from the sap of trees in Malaya, made a good insulator. Cables under the sea – submarine cables – were now possible. On 28 August 1850 a steam tug laid a single copper wire insulated with gutta percha across the Channel. For a

few hours that evening messages were exchanged between France and England. But a fisherman picked up the cable in his nets. He thought it was some strange kind of seaweed, or a sea monster, and cut a piece out of the cable to show his friends!

Next year the engineers tried again and this time they protected the cable with thick iron wires. It was a success and remained in use for several years. Its success led to many other cables being laid, but the biggest challenge – the Atlantic – still had to be met.

Cables across the Atlantic
Both the technology and the money to build submarine cables were now available. In the middle of the 1800s the British Empire was at its peak. Trade was flourishing. Bankers, merchants and businessmen were willing to invest a great deal of money in return for better information.

It was an American, Cyrus Field, who persuaded the merchants and bankers of Manchester, Liverpool and London to invest in his project to lay a submarine cable across the Atlantic. The attempt took place in 1858. Two ships were needed to carry the cable. They worked in some of the worst storms experienced in the Atlantic. Eventually the cable was laid and Queen Victoria and the

Cable for controlling Seadog from the surface.

Sand and water from the trench being pumped away.

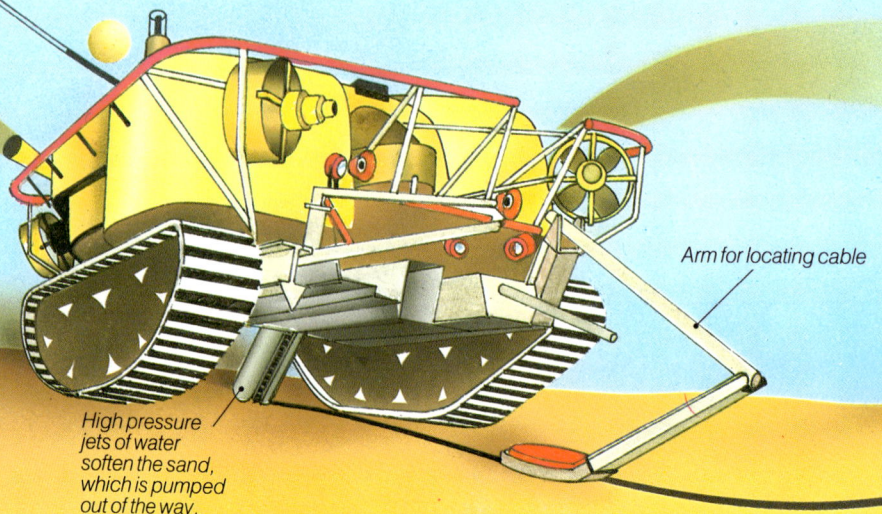

Below: Cables on the sea bed are buffeted by the sea and worn away by shifting sands. Also they must be protected from ships' anchors and fishing nets. One of the best ways of protecting the cables is to bury them.

Arm for locating cable

High pressure jets of water soften the sand, which is pumped out of the way.

President of the United States, President Buchanan, exchanged messages on 13 August 1858.

There were however some major unforeseen problems and a few weeks later the cable broke down and refused to work again. Field and his investors were not daunted. After several years, they hired the *Great Eastern*, the largest ship afloat, to carry all 3,700 km of cable in her specially converted holds. In 1865 the *Great Eastern* had laid about half of the cable when the cable broke and it could not be retrieved from the bottom of the sea. Next year the *Great Eastern* set out again and successfully laid a submarine cable across the Atlantic. She also retrieved the lost end of the first cable, spliced a new piece of cable onto the end and completed the line. So in 1866 there were two working submarine cables under the Atlantic.

This triumph stimulated the spread of telegraphy over the whole world. By the turn of the century it was possible to send a message practically anywhere by using the world-wide network of land lines and submarine cables. The cost of sending a telegram was also reduced considerably and by 1885, 90 million telegrams were being sent annually.

Since the cables were so long the signals were very weak by the time they reached the other side. Very sensitive pieces of equipment were designed and built to detect these weak signals.

Submarine telegraph cables flourished until well into the 1950s. They were finally put out of action by the arrival of submarine telephone cables. Speech signals need to be amplified about every 35 km. Repeaters were designed and built to amplify these weak signals and pass them on.

Cables are still being laid under the sea. But they are now very different from the early ones. Coaxial cables and optical fibres are the new technologies which have now ousted the plain copper wire cables.

Below: Early optical fibre cables, such as that laid in Loch Fyne, Scotland, during 1980, have up to five pairs of optical fibres. Each pair has a capacity of 1,920 circuits.

Below: A coaxial cable has a central conductor. This is surrounded by an insulator and then an outer cylindrical conductor. This type of modern coaxial cable has the capacity of 4,000 circuits.

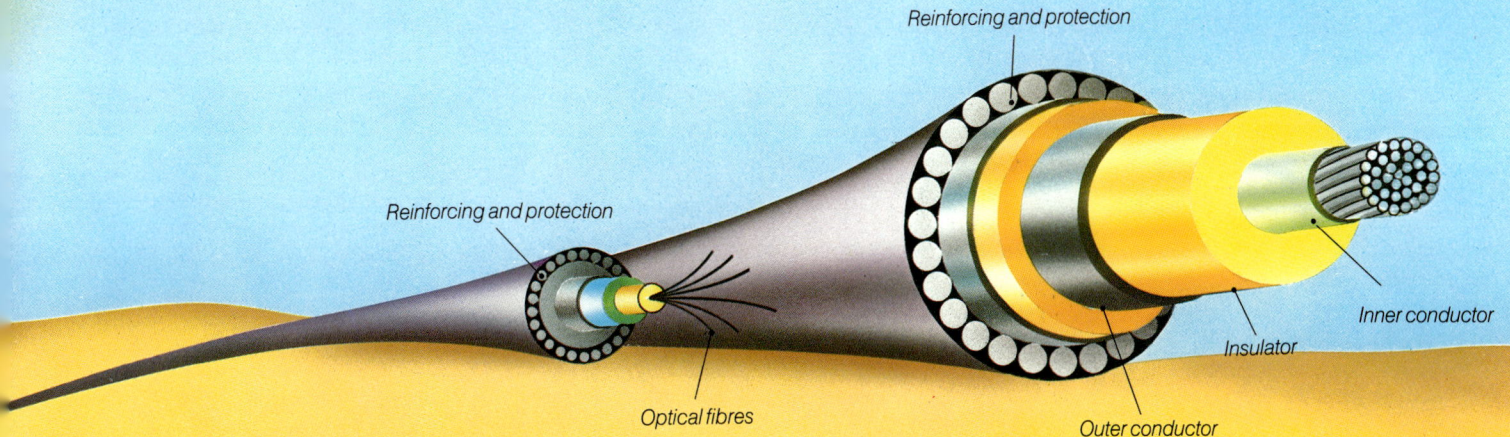

Reinforcing and protection

Reinforcing and protection

Inner conductor

Insulator

Optical fibres

Outer conductor

First telephones

When you speak the vocal chords in your throat vibrate. This causes tiny changes in the pressure of the air, and sound waves radiate from your mouth. When you listen to someone talk, the sound waves coming from the person's mouth enter your ear. The small pressure changes are converted into nerve signals which are sent to your brain. But air does not transmit sound waves very well over a distance, so some other way is needed.

It was Robert Hooke in 1667 who first suggested the string telephone. Most people have connected two tins by a taut piece of string and sent messages over it. However, it is not a very practical device and does not work over long distances.

Alexander Graham Bell

Two Americans, working independently of each other, invented telephones at the same time. We remember Alexander Graham Bell as the inventor of the telephone because he got to the Patent Office a few hours before Elisha Gray on 14 February 1876. Bell brought together the work of several scientists to produce the telephone.

Bell based his telephone on the electromagnet. He used two of them joined together by two wires. This worked but it was not very efficient. However, it was the invention of the carbon microphone that ensured the early success of the telephone.

When you speak into the microphone of the telephone, the sound waves from your mouth make a diaphragm vibrate. The diaphragm presses on to carbon granules and this affects the electric current that flows through them. The diagram on the opposite page shows you what a diaphragm and carbon microphone look like.

The microphone turns the changes in the sound waves into changes in electric current. This electric current is fed down a pair of wires to the receiving telephone. Here the fluctuating current passes through the coil of wire and makes the diaphragm vibrate. This reproduces the sound waves which entered the microphone.

Above: L.M. Ericsson introduced the first table telephone in 1892. It is considered to be a fine example of mechanical engineering as every part has a purpose.

Early problems

Bell promoted his telephone very actively. He talked and demonstrated it all over America and also in England. Due to Bell's efforts the development of the telephone was rapid in America. However, in some other countries, such as England and France, people were not so enthusiastic about the telephone. They preferred to use messenger boys. The sound quality of the telephone was poor, it did not work over long distances and it was very expensive. In 1878, the cost of connecting two offices with telephones was more than a year's wages for a servant. A lot of money had been invested in the telegraph system and the investors obviously did not want to encourage something which would destroy their business.

Telephones had to be connected by pairs of wires. Since they were to carry speech they had to be of a higher quality than telegraph lines. The wires were carried overhead from poles. But they were likely to be blown down by gales or brought down in winter by the weight of sleet and snow freezing them. It is better if the wires are underground and out of sight, but underground cables were more expensive.

Left: Where there were many lines derricks were erected to carry all the wires. Such aerial chaos now no longer exists.

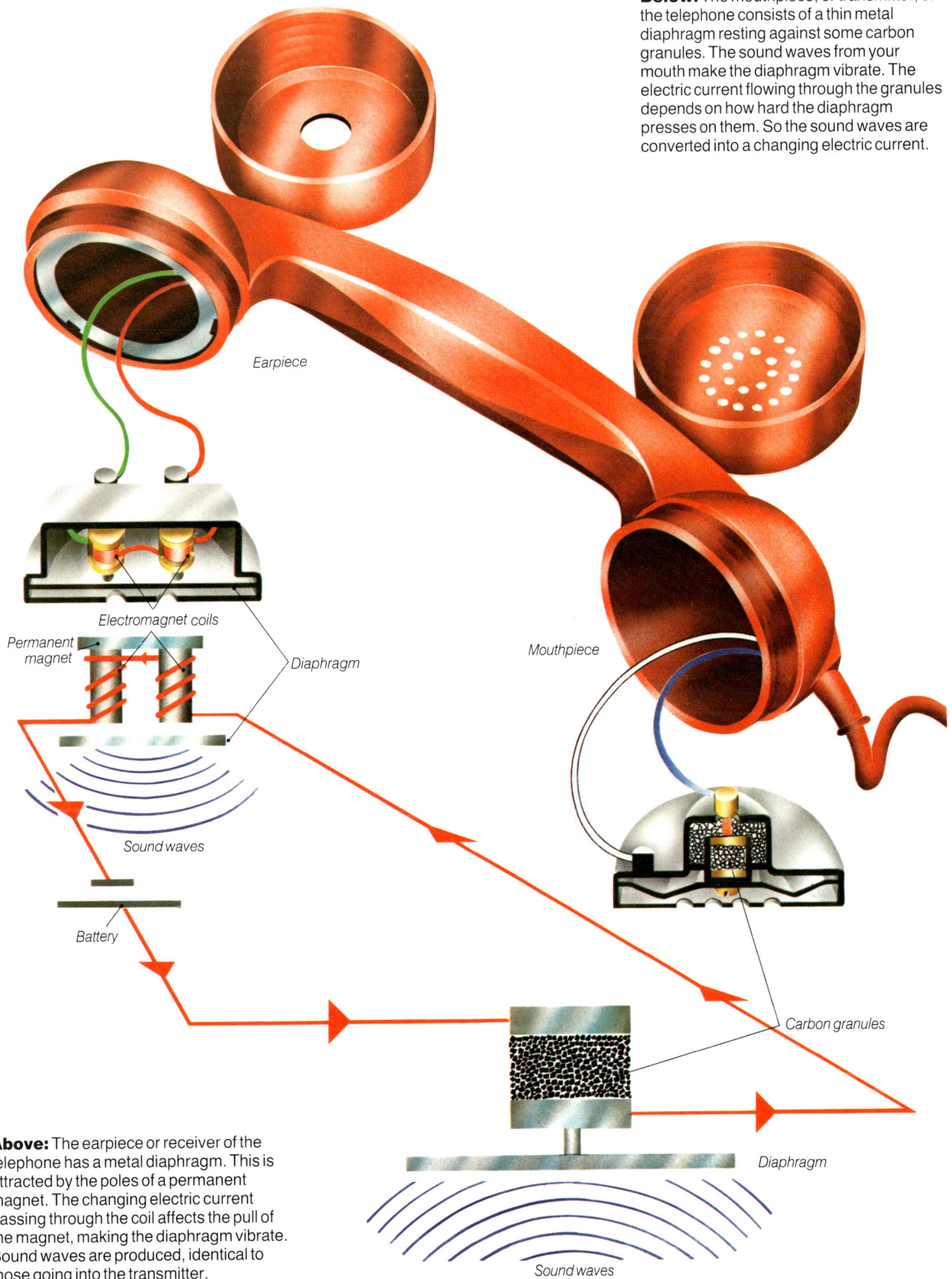

Below: The mouthpiece, or transmitter, of the telephone consists of a thin metal diaphragm resting against some carbon granules. The sound waves from your mouth make the diaphragm vibrate. The electric current flowing through the granules depends on how hard the diaphragm presses on them. So the sound waves are converted into a changing electric current.

Earpiece

Electromagnet coils

Permanent magnet

Diaphragm

Mouthpiece

Sound waves

Battery

Carbon granules

Diaphragm

Above: The earpiece or receiver of the telephone has a metal diaphragm. This is attracted by the poles of a permanent magnet. The changing electric current passing through the coil affects the pull of the magnet, making the diaphragm vibrate. Sound waves are produced, identical to those going into the transmitter.

Sound waves

15

Telephone exchanges

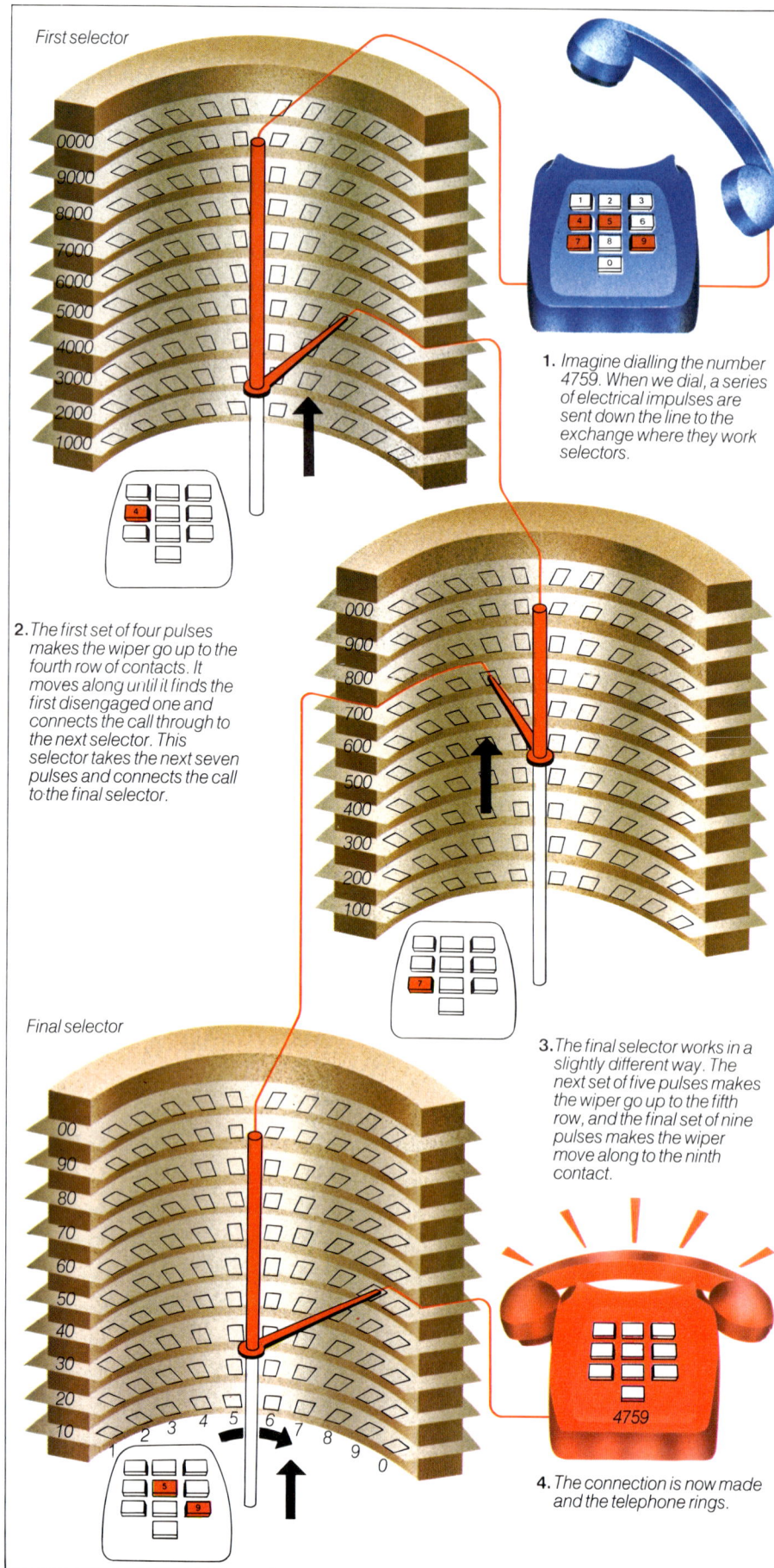

First selector

0000
9000
8000
7000
6000
5000
4000
3000
2000
1000

1. *Imagine dialling the number 4759. When we dial, a series of electrical impulses are sent down the line to the exchange where they work selectors.*

2. *The first set of four pulses makes the wiper go up to the fourth row of contacts. It moves along until it finds the first disengaged one and connects the call through to the next selector. This selector takes the next seven pulses and connects the call to the final selector.*

000
900
800
700
600
500
400
300
200
100

3. *The final selector works in a slightly different way. The next set of five pulses makes the wiper go up to the fifth row, and the final set of nine pulses makes the wiper move along to the ninth contact.*

Final selector

00
90
80
70
60
50
40
30
20
10

1 2 3 4 5 6 7 8 9 0

4759

4. *The connection is now made and the telephone rings.*

At first the telephone just linked two houses, or offices, together. You actually bought the telephone and had your own private line. There was no way of connecting your pair of telephones to another pair. Obviously, this was not very convenient, so very quickly exchanges were built and installed to enable this to happen. The first exchanges were operated by people, called operators.

Manual exchanges

Each operator sat in front of a switchboard, similar to the ones in the photograph. At first, only a few people had telephones. The line from each telephone ended on this board with a socket. When you wanted to make a call, you turned the handle on the side of the telephone and an electric current was generated. This electric current travelled along the wires and made an indicator move on the operator's board. The operator then plugged a cord into your socket and asked you the number you wanted. Then the operator connected you to that number by joining your socket to the number you asked for by a lead with a plug on each end. Each operator could handle about 50 lines.

Small manual switchboards were fine when there were few subscribers. The first telephone directory ever issued was in New Haven, Connecticut, USA in February 1878. It was all on one piece of paper – on one side!

At first, most of the telephones were owned by businesses, because the rental was high. The charge for a telephone was fixed, but you could make as many calls as you wished. This made it expensive for ordinary people.

During the 1880s many more people began to have telephones, and so multiple exchanges were developed and installed to cope with the increased number of calls. These gave each operator access to all the lines leaving the exchange, not just the lines on their particular switchboard.

Automatic exchanges

Almon B. Strowger was an undertaker. He thought that he was getting poor telephone service from his local manual exchange. He also thought that the operator was directing business away from him. So he invented an automatic exchange and patented it in 1891. Each

Left: Making a telephone call through an automatic exchange.

Above: Originally telephones did not have dials. Only when automatic exchanges came into use was it necessary to have a telephone with a dial. These first dials had both numbers and letters.

telephone had to have a way of telling the automatic exchange which number it wanted. This was done by the dial. When you dialled a number, a series of electrical impulses were sent to the exchange. These operated the special switches (selectors) which connected you with the phone you wanted.

The world's first automatic exchange was installed at La Porte, Indiana in 1892, but Strowger's marvellous invention was slow to spread. Seventeen years passed before the first automatic exchange was opened in Europe at Munich. In England it was not until 1958, when the first Subscriber Trunk Dialling (STD) exchange was opened in Bristol, that you could dial from one city to another. Before this time you had to call the operator to connect you. Now we take for granted the fact that we can dial directly to people in most countries of the world, by dialling no more than 14 digits.

Crossbar

Many improvements have been made in telephone exchanges and different systems tried. One of the most successful is called the crossbar system. This is also an electromechanical system but is able to handle more calls at once.

Electronic exchanges

Nowadays, engineers are working on developing purely electronic exchanges using microchips which have no moving parts at all. Many things which could not be done on a manual exchange have now become possible, by using such electronic exchanges. For instance, we can now have conference calls or use abbreviated dialling.

Above: The Royal Exchange, Manchester, in 1895. In the early days of telephone exchanges many women became telephone operators. It was one of the first acceptable jobs for a woman.

Below: Contrast the manual exchange with the modern digital trunk exchange made by Standard Elektrik Lorenz AG, Stuttgart. This exchange is now in operation in Munich.

Growth of telephones

Below: Making a trunk call: all long distance calls begin with a '0'. This '0' tells the equipment at the local exchange that it is a trunk call. Special equipment stores the numbers, works out where the call is going, and routes the call through to the distant exchange. The local exchange also keeps a record of the cost of the call.

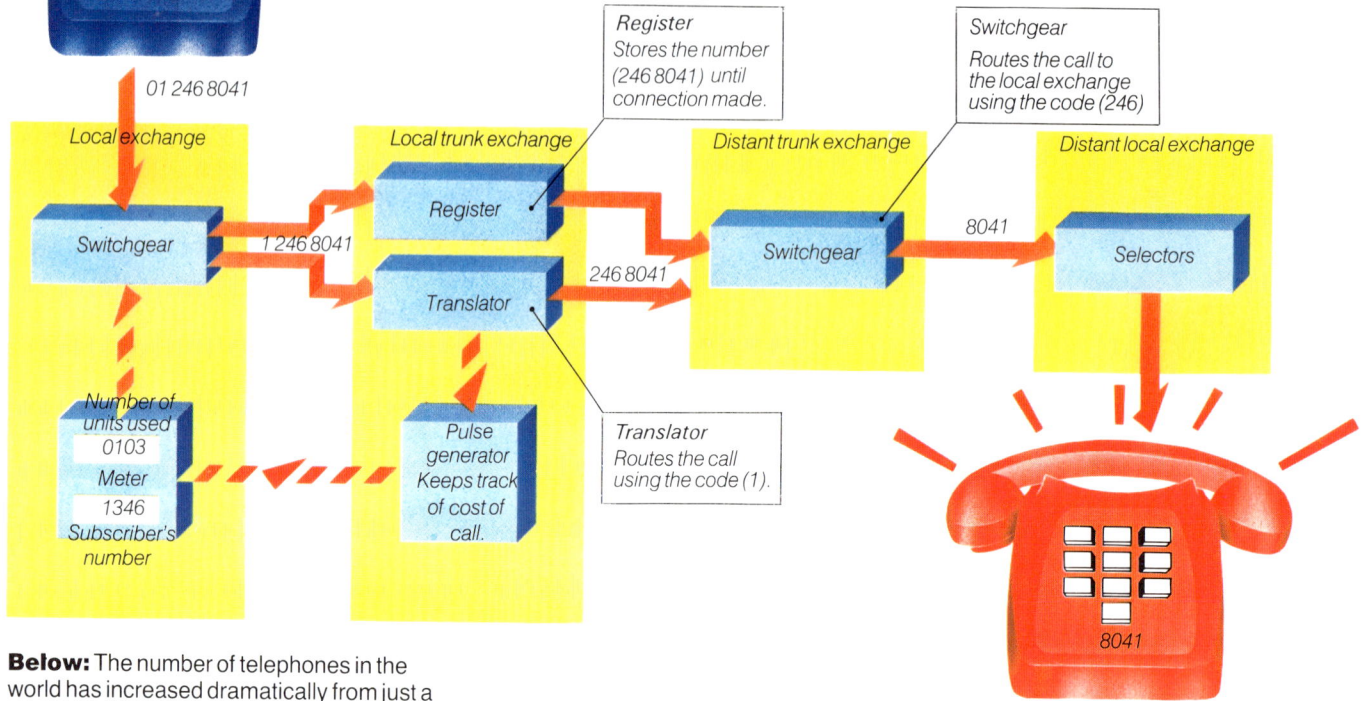

01 246 8041

Local exchange

Switchgear

1 246 8041

Number of units used
0103
Meter
1346
Subscriber's number

Local trunk exchange

Register

Translator

Pulse generator
Keeps track of cost of call.

Register
Stores the number (246 8041) until connection made.

Translator
Routes the call using the code (1).

246 8041

Distant trunk exchange

Switchgear

Switchgear
Routes the call to the local exchange using the code (246)

8041

Distant local exchange

Selectors

8041

Below: The number of telephones in the world has increased dramatically from just a few thousand, when they were first invented, to many hundreds of millions today.

Number of telephones in the world

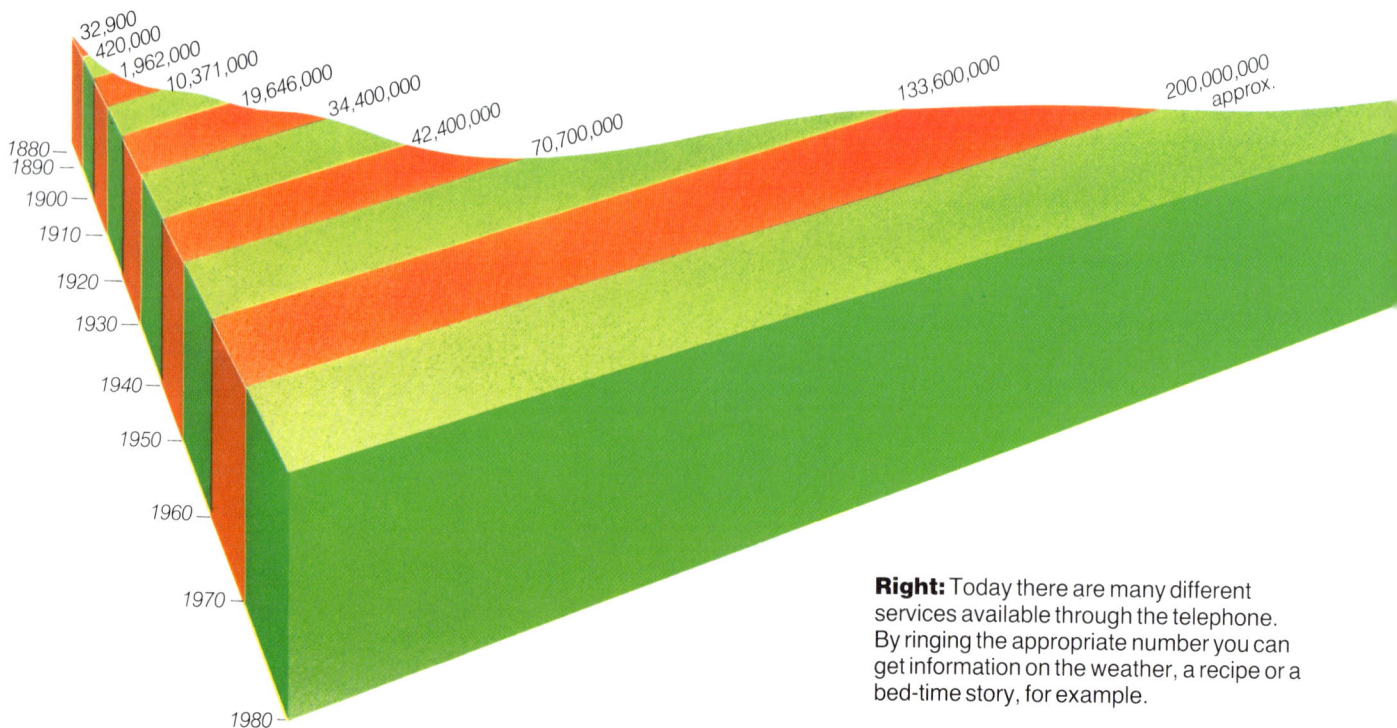

32,900
420,000
1,962,000
10,371,000
19,646,000
34,400,000
42,400,000
70,700,000
133,600,000
200,000,000 approx.

1880
1890
1900
1910
1920
1930
1940
1950
1960
1970
1980

Right: Today there are many different services available through the telephone. By ringing the appropriate number you can get information on the weather, a recipe or a bed-time story, for example.

On 1 January 1877 there were just 2,600 telephones in the world. Twenty years later there were over a million. Another twenty years later there were over 17 million. This is very rapid growth. As more and more people used the telephone they demanded better services and more improvements. For example, callers wanted to talk easily to people a long way away.

Long distance wires

Thick heavy copper wires were used on the long-distance lines. Thick wire was used to preserve the strength of the signals. Therefore a mile of the wire weighed 273 kg, and massive poles were needed to support these wires. As copper was not cheap the lines were expensive to build.

As the length of a telephone line increases, the quality of the speech received becomes muffled until it becomes completely unintelligible. To prevent this from happening, devices called loading coils were put into telephone circuits about the turn of the century. Loading coils couldn't strengthen the signals at all, but they could keep the losses of quality along the wire to a minimum. This meant that the quality of long distance calls was improved.

Clearly a means had to be found to strengthen the weak signals and pass them on at full strength. Repeaters were developed to do just this. Wires could now be much thinner and put underground.

Subscriber Trunk Dialling (STD)

During the 1930s the telephone began to be used by the ordinary person. As more and more people used the telephone the charges fell.

In 1932 it became easier to make a long distance or trunk call. Instead of having to book the call, and perhaps have to wait up to an hour, it was now possible to be connected straight away. Many years passed before it was possible to dial a trunk call yourself. On 5 December 1958 the Queen officially opened the first automatic exchange in Bristol. STD – Subscriber Trunk Dialling – had started. It took 21 years to convert all exchanges to automatic working. In 1963 a call from London to Paris marked the start of International Direct Dialling (IDD). Today we can dial direct to over 100 countries, about nine-tenths of the world's total.

One problem that automatic dialling created was how to charge and bill customers for the calls they made. When operators connected the calls, they made a note of the length of the call and the distance. It was then easy to work out the cost. With the introduction of STD special equipment had to be designed and built to do this automatically.

Telephone services

London's speaking clock started in 1936. And the use of 999 for emergency services became available in London in 1937. This was, and is, free.

As STD spread, operators became free to offer more assistance to their customers. They provided help in finding numbers (directory enquiries) and more recently, now look after credit card calls, for instance.

Radio-telephones

Even if you are driving along in a car it is possible for someone to ring you up. In certain areas there is a radio-telephone system which is connected to the STD network. Dialling a special code and then the person's number can put you in touch with someone on the move.

In fact, radio-telephone links have been in existence for over 55 years. Radio waves in the high frequency band (4-30 MHz) were used for the intercontinental links. As submarine cables and satellites developed and improved, they have taken over the high frequency radio links.

Voices over the air

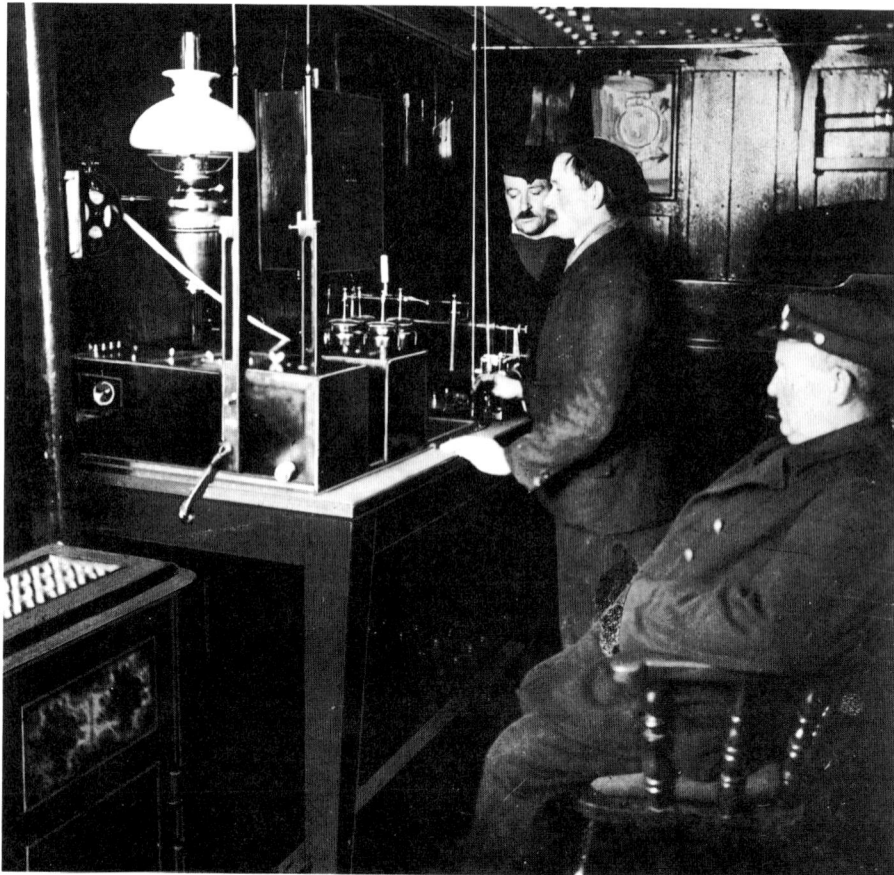

In 1864 James Clerk Maxwell used mathematics to predict that there were such things as radio waves. He worked out their speed and showed that these waves were similar to light waves. He said that you could reflect and refract them as you could light waves. But you could not see them or feel them. These remarkable claims were rejected by other scientists who could not understand or appreciate Maxwell's mathematics. He died before his brilliant piece of work received the recognition it deserved.

Over twenty years later in 1887, Heinrich Hertz, a German scientist, showed

Left: In 1898 the East Goodwin Lightship had a wireless installed. A short while later a steamer ran into the lightship. The accident was immediately reported to the shore and as a result no lives were lost.

Below: Marconi (fourth from the right) is seen here demonstrating his radio equipment to the Italian navy in 1897. The Italian government showed little interest in Marconi's early work and he came to England to raise money to set up his own wireless telegraph company.

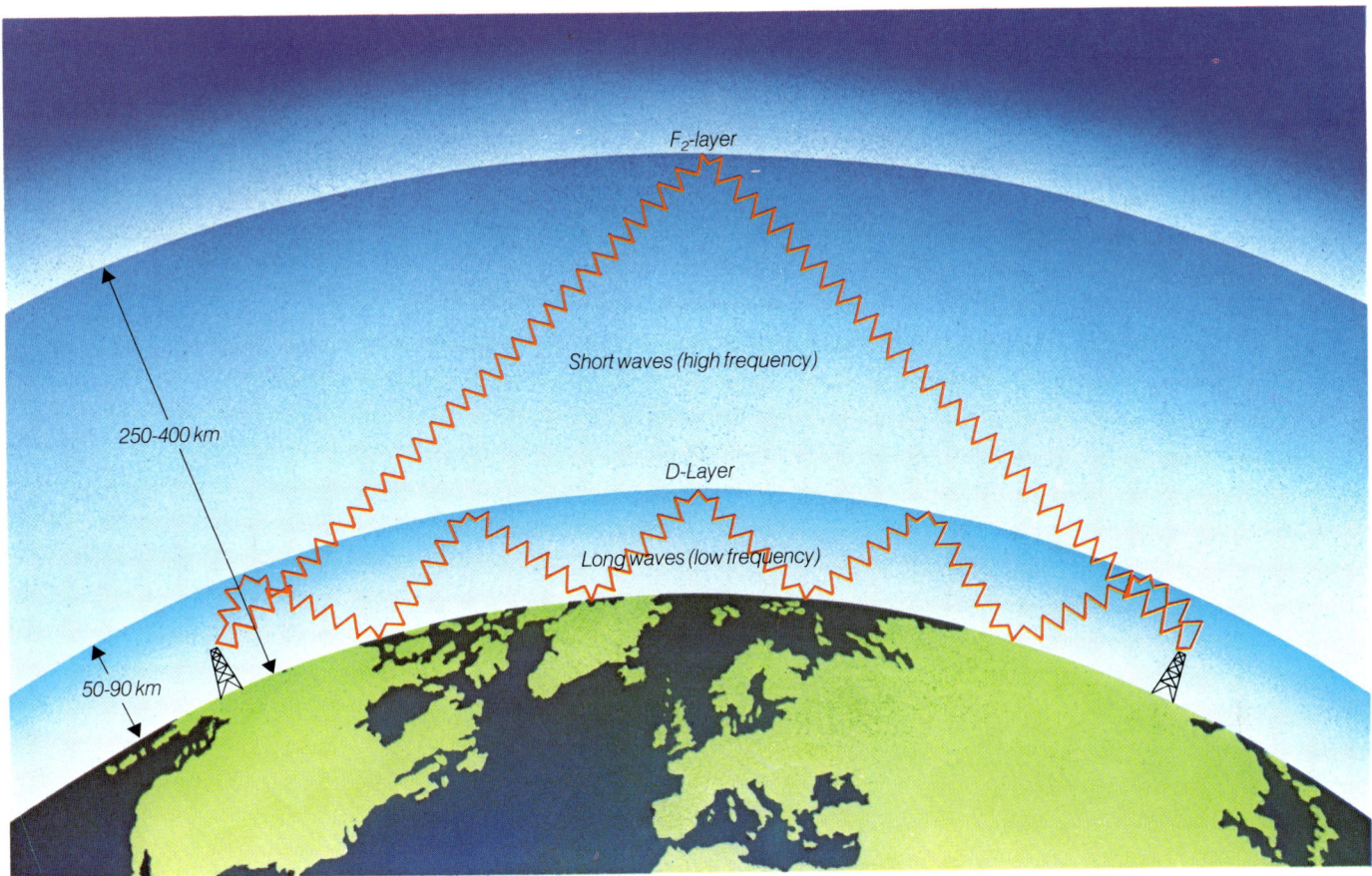

F₂-layer

Short waves (high frequency)

250-400 km

D-Layer

Long waves (low frequency)

50-90 km

that radio waves did exist. Also, they could be reflected, bent and twisted just as Maxwell had predicted. Many scientists played about with these radio waves. They were just a curiosity. No-one believed or realised how useful they could be.

Guglielmo Marconi

It was Guglielmo Marconi who turned scientific toys into a fully practical system. He was an ingenious and brilliant engineer. In 1896, he demonstrated his simple but effective apparatus for transmitting radio waves to William Preece, the chief engineer of the Post Office in England. Preece was enthusiastic and arranged for Marconi to demonstrate to government officials and officers in the armed services. Everyone was impressed by Marconi's equipment and its potential.

William Preece tried to get the British government to finance Marconi. But the government could not make up its mind quickly enough. They soon bitterly regretted their lack of decision. Marconi formed Marconi's Wireless Telegraph Company to promote his work. It made him a fortune, and today is still a highly successful company.

Wireless telegraphy

Wireless telegraphy was aptly named – no wires were used to connect the sender and receiver. To make the radio waves electric sparks were used. A lot of electric interference today is caused by sparks. They produce the crackling noise we hear on radios. The sparks may come from an electric motor, for example; or from a switch turning an electric light on or off.

On 12 December 1901 Marconi proved many scientists wrong by transmitting a radio message from Cornwall, England to Newfoundland, Canada. Radio waves had travelled a distance of 3,440 km. They arrived despite the curvature of the Earth.

Wireless telegraphy was very suitable for communicating with ships. In 1910, a sensational news item showed the potential of wireless. On the liner *Montrose*, the captain noticed that one of his passengers was Dr. Crippen, an infamous murderer who was fleeing to Canada from England. The ship had a spark transmitter. Using morse code the wireless operator sent a message to Scotland Yard telling of Crippen's presence in disguise on the ship. A detective boarded a faster ship and managed to

Above: There are several layers of the Earth's atmosphere which can reflect radio waves. High frequency waves (short waves) are reflected by the ionized F₂-layer, and low frequency waves (long waves) by the D-layer. Thus radio waves can defeat the Earth's curvature.

get to Canada before the *Montrose*. Because of the wireless messages, Crippen was arrested.

Crippen's life at sea was described in the newspapers. Regular dispatches were sent from the ship to England. Crippen was completely unaware that he was making the headlines. He thought he was free – but the wireless beat him.

Two years later, in 1912, the *Titanic* sank with a huge loss of life after hitting an iceberg. The *Titanic* had a wireless set and had sent off a distress signal. The nearest ship also had a wireless, but did not hear the call for help. It had only one operator and since he had been on duty for 18 hours, he was having a rest. Many more lives would have been saved if this ship had heard the distress call and other ships had had wireless sets. There was a huge outcry. Legislation was introduced to require ships to carry a wireless and to listen at all times for distress calls.

Radio for entertainment

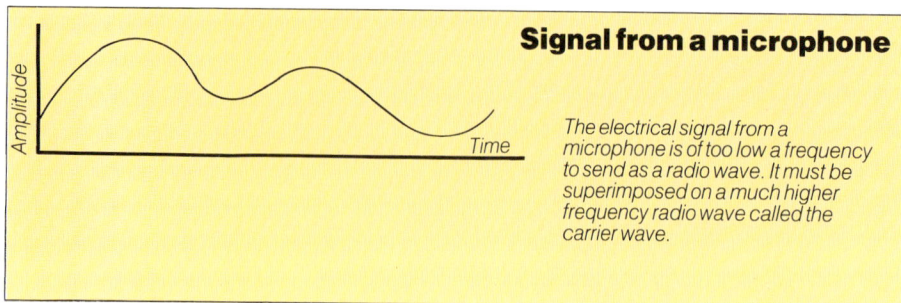

Signal from a microphone

Amplitude / Time

The electrical signal from a microphone is of too low a frequency to send as a radio wave. It must be superimposed on a much higher frequency radio wave called the carrier wave.

Amplitude modulation

Background noise
Amplitude / Time
Carrier wave

Amplitude Modulation (AM): The strength, or amplitude, of the carrier varies in the same way as the original signal. A disadvantage is that quiet parts of the signal can be drowned by background noise.

Frequency modulation

Background noise
Amplitude / Time
Carrier wave

Frequency modulation (FM): The frequency of the carrier varies in the same way as the original signal. For high quality, FM is used.

Just before Christmas 1906 many wireless operators were astonished to hear music coming through their headphones instead of morse code. R. A. Fessenden had managed to transmit music and speech a distance of over 300 km. But many years were to pass before radio broadcasting as we know it became possible, with the invention of the thermionic valve.

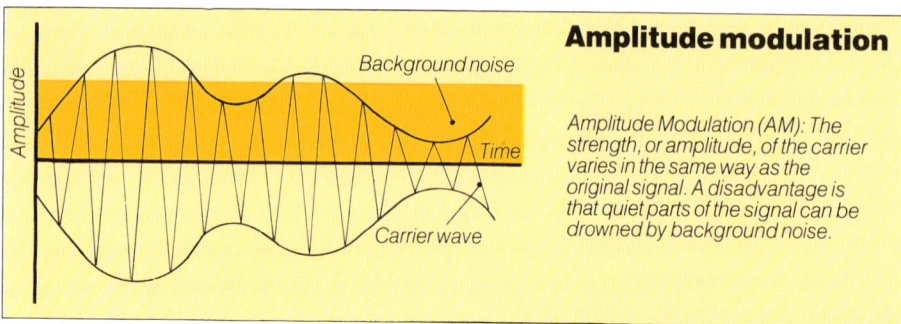

Right from the beginning enthusiastic amateurs have built wireless receivers and transmitters and used them to communicate with one another. Various frequencies were set aside for them to use, away from commercial users. The idea of using the radio to provide entertainment was novel. Some experimenters in Europe began to liven up their transmissions with improvised entertainment. The amateurs loved it and wanted more. The makers of radio receivers began to appreciate how big the demand was, and decided to broadcast entertainment themselves.

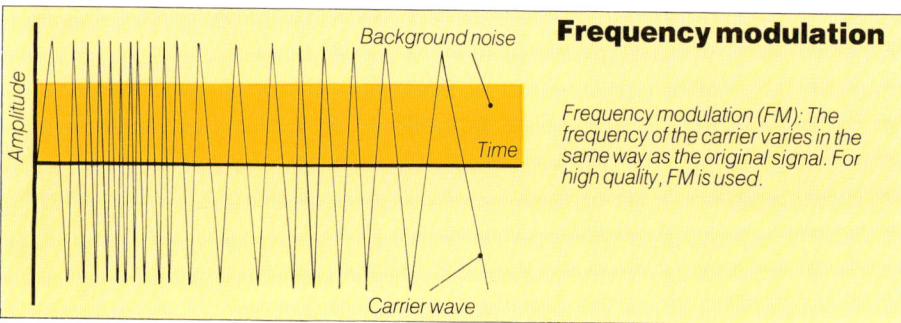

This caused problems though, as the transmissions sometimes interfered with ordinary radio communication. To begin with amateurs were allowed to broadcast for fifteen minutes during a weekly half an hour slot. There had to be many compulsory breaks though, to listen out for messages which were more important.

The first radio stations

In 1922, in England, there was a meeting to discuss how to organise the broadcasting system. Eventually it was agreed to form the British Broadcasting Company (BBC). It would receive its income

Below: J.A. Fleming invented the thermionic valve in 1904. This is a device which only conducts electricity in one direction. It can be used to detect high frequency radio waves.

Below: A cheap alternative to the valve was the 'cat's whisker'. It was a small spring resting on a crystal of carborundum or galena. With a few other cheap components you could make a 'crystal set'.

In the early days of radio, recording was difficult so the vast majority of programmes were broadcast live. This made broadcasting very exciting, especially if sound effects were required.

from a radio licence and from a royalty on receivers. This was different from the American radio stations which used advertising to provide them with income.

The BBC broadcast its first programme on 14 November 1922. A year later enough stations were in operation for about 50% of the population in Great Britain to receive broadcasts on a crystal set, which was one of the first kinds of radio receiver.

Each station had its own studio and produced its own programmes. Clearly, it would be a great help if the stations could share programmes. So ways of linking stations together were tried. Ordinary telephone lines could be used but this tended to disrupt the whole telephone network. Special lines and links had to be built.

Most broadcasting took place on the medium waveband (from 500 kHz to 1500 kHz). The main disadvantage was that these waves do not travel over the horizon. Long radio waves were used to transmit to people a long way away as they can be bent by the Earth's atmosphere. But very powerful transmitters were needed to send out long radio waves.

Short waveband

Amateurs were only allowed to experiment on the short waveband, as the authorities thought that it wasn't very useful for communication. But the amateurs confounded the experts by showing that short waves could be used to communicate with people the other side of the world. Also the transmitters they used did not have to be nearly as

powerful as the ones used for broadcasting on the long waveband. Soon the Marconi Company established a network of short-wave 'beam' stations. These short waves could be beamed to different parts of the world by reflecting them off the ionosphere.

Many things which we now take for granted had to be invented. Microphones had to be developed which could accurately transform speech and music into electrical signals. Studios were built which could keep out all other noises apart from the ones which were supposed to be transmitted. Until 1930 everything that was broadcast was live.

Improvements in valve radio receivers meant that several radio stations could broadcast on frequencies which were fairly close together. This was the beginning of the end for the crystal set.

23

At war

Below: By 1939 a series of radar stations had been set up around Britain's coast. Instead of patrolling the coast constantly, aircraft could remain on the ground until radar indicated the approach of enemy aircraft. Fighters were then 'scrambled' to meet them.

The Second World War was different from other wars. It was not just people with weapons fighting one another. Scientists were battling it out too. Some say that it was the outcome of the battle between the scientists which decided who won the war. We shall look at a few developments of radio about 50 years ago which started this war of electronics.

Radar (Radio direction and ranging)

During the 1930s scientists were asked if it was possible to build some kind of a 'death ray' using radio waves. Calculation soon showed that this was impossible, but that detection of ships and planes might be possible. Quickly the idea was tried out and found to work.

The radar transmitter sends out a stream of pulses of radio waves. If an aircraft gets in the way it reflects the pulse back to the transmitter. Obviously the longer it takes for a reflected pulse to return, the further away is the aircraft. The echo is displayed on a cathode-ray screen which is like the one used in a television set. The height of an aircraft can also be measured.

Radio direction finding

One way of navigating is to use radio beacons. These are the radio equivalent of the lighthouse. The beacon sends out a signal in all directions. By using a special movable aerial it is possible to find out where the signal is coming from. Using two beacons it is possible to plot your position. Sailors and airmen still use this system today.

Knickebein

Before the war a system called 'Lorenz' existed to guide aircraft back to airfields in the dark or in bad weather. Experts said that it would not work over greater distances than about 50 km.

However, British intelligence reports suggested that the German scientists had developed a system, called Knickebein, to guide bombers to their target over much longer distances. Many people were sceptical, but it was soon found that the reports were true.

Immediately, a new unit was formed to counter Knickebein. Jammers had to be built. These transmitted a signal on the same frequency to confuse the German receivers. Amazingly it was a piece of hospital equipment called a diathermy set that was rapidly converted into a jammer. It was the only piece of equipment, at the time, that could generate radio waves at the right frequency – about 30 MHz at high power.

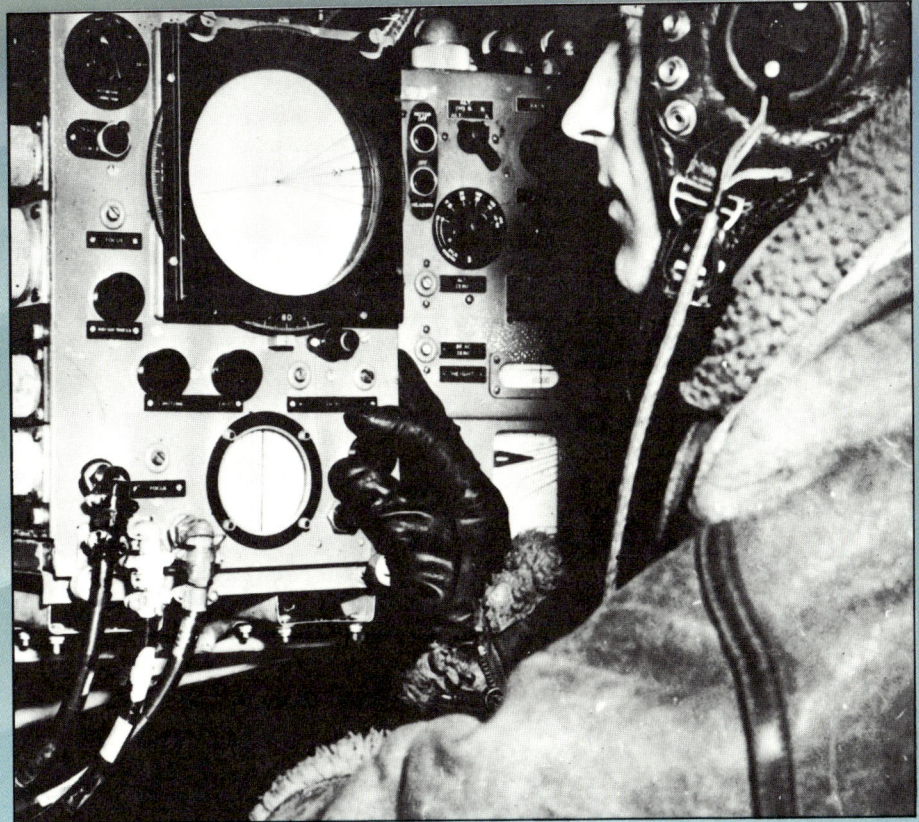

X-Gerät

As soon as the German scientists real-ised that Knickebein was being success-fully jammed, they devised a new sys-tem called X-Gerät. This was much more effective. The British scientists found it difficult to jam successfully. Very skilled German pilots used X-Gerät to find their target, where they dropped incendiary bombs to start fires to guide the bombers. The best counter measure was very simple – fires were started in the country to try and create confusion.

Airborne radar

To enable planes to detect small objects on the ground or sea, extremely high frequency radio waves had to be used. Ordinary valves could not produce radio waves of this frequency. A device called a magnetron was invented, which produced powerful bursts of high fre-quency waves.

When war ended

Many of the developments made during the war led to improvements in the peacetime use of telecommunications. For example, LORAN, a navigation sys-tem for sailors and airmen, is still in use today. Radar and the other navigational aids make travelling by air and sea safe.

Above: Radar sets were quickly developed which could detect ships and submarines on the surface of the sea and were small enough to fit inside an aircraft. They were also used to direct guns to their target.

Below: Radio made it easy to communicate with soldiers in the field, planes, and spies! But everyone else could listen in as well – this made sending secrets difficult and dangerous.

Television appears

Over one hundred years ago, telegraphs had been invented which could send a photograph over a wire. These devices worked by 'scanning' the photograph, breaking it up into spots, and sending information about each spot one after the other along the wire. This was very slow as a picture had to be broken up into many thousands of dots. Sending moving pictures was a challenge to many scientists.

A television picture is made by a spot of light moving rapidly across the screen of a cathode-ray tube. It traces out several hundred 'lines' as it moves from top to bottom of the screen. Since the spot moves so quickly the picture appears steady. It was the invention of the cathode-ray tube in 1897 that sparked off several ideas for using it as the display part of a television.

These ideas were beyond the capability of the technology at that time. But by the 1920s many devices were available which were of great help to those experimenting with television. There were better photo-cells, valve amplifiers and much experience of radio transmitters and receivers.

But it was the camera which caused the biggest problem. A camera has to scan the picture to be sent, and convert it into electrical signals. These are then sent along wires, or through the air, to the receiver. The first scanning device was a mechanical one, patented by a German student, Nipkow, in 1883.

John Logie Baird

In England, John Logie Baird also worked on this idea. In 1925, he demonstrated his mechanical scanning device, which was based on Nipkow's invention. It was a tremendous achievement and a lot of public interest was shown in his invention. Over the next ten years, Baird and his company spent a great deal of effort improving their system.

However, a rival electronic system was developed in the 1930s. In America, Vladimir Zworykin had invented the first electronic camera tube, which was called an iconoscope. This used a beam of electrons as a scanning device. EMI (Electronic and Musical Industries) decided to use Zworykin's iconoscope in their television camera.

Below: A television camera (iconoscope) works in the following way. The camera lens focuses the picture onto a mosaic screen of caesium dots. The brighter the light on each dot, the more electrical charge builds up on it. To release the charge the screen is scanned by a beam of electrons. The picture is thus turned into little pulses of electricity.

In the receiver these little pulses vary the strength of an electron beam as it scans the screen, faithfully reproducing the original picture.

Iconoscope

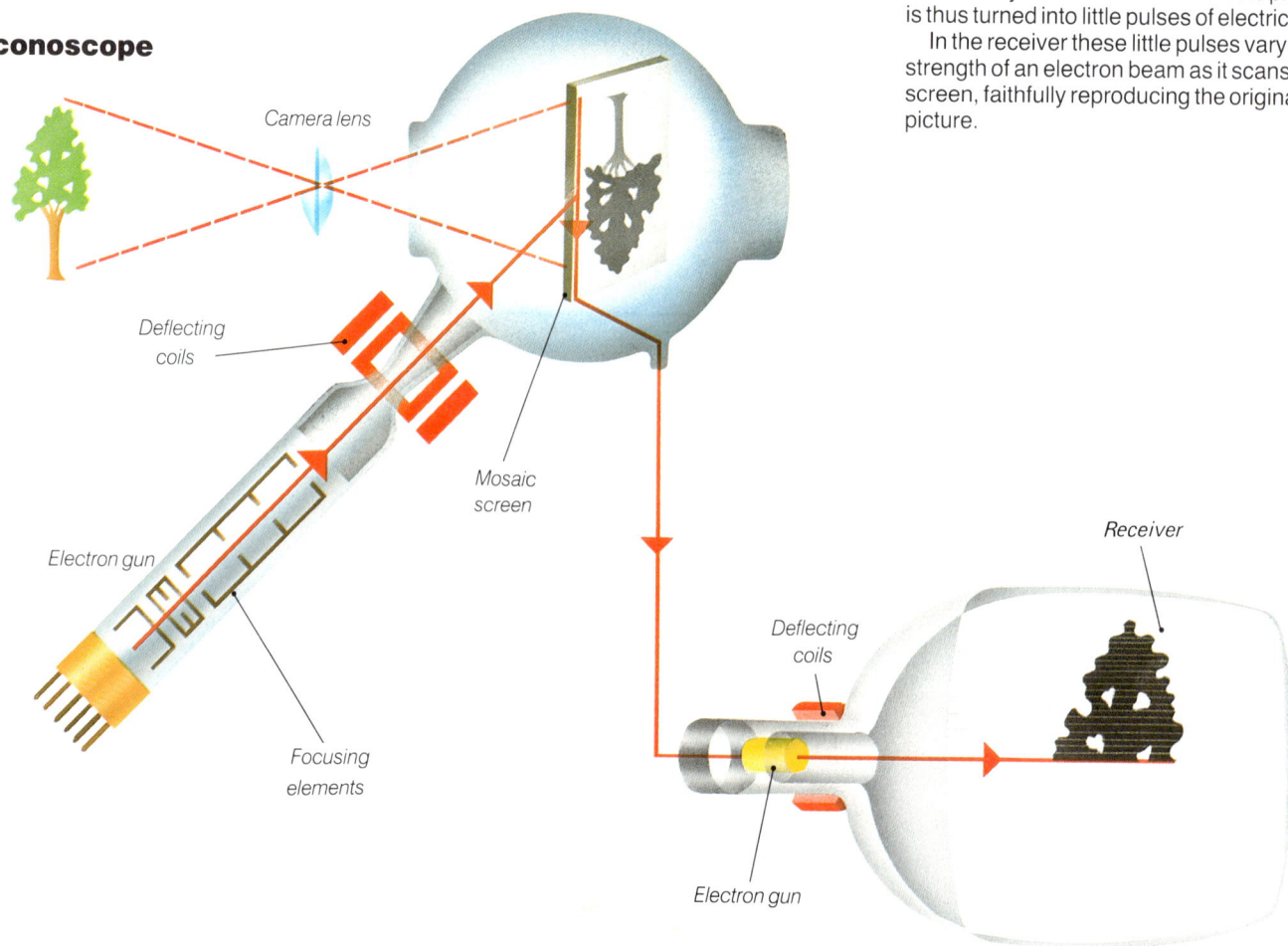

Right: The world's first high definition television studios were at Alexandra Palace, London. A 1936 camera is in the foreground and the large transmitting aerial in the background.

Left: The tube in this 1930's television set is mounted vertically because it is so long. On the lid is a mirror so that you can see the picture when you are sitting down.

To transmit a better picture, and sound as well, required a bigger bandwidth. Both companies had to explore transmitting in the VHF (very high frequency) waveband, as space was not available on the medium waveband. The authorities waited until the experimenters were able to show they had a really effective television system before allowing them any of the valuable space on the existing wavebands. Then, the two systems of television were given a trial run.

Regular transmission begins

On 2 November 1936, the BBC's television service started, the first in the world. To begin with, each system was used on alternate weeks. It soon became apparent that the electronic system was better than the mechanical one, and the BBC adopted the 405-line system of EMI/Marconi as standard.

Television received a lot of publicity. But by the end of 1937 fewer than 2,000 receivers had been sold. There were several reasons for this. One was that the receivers were very expensive – about half the price of a small car. People thought that better receivers would soon be available at a reduced price. Secondly, there were only two hours of television broadcast each day (from 3 to 4 during the afternoon and from 9 to 10 at night).

When the Second World War broke out in 1939 the television service was suspended. It did not start up again until June 1946. It attracted little attention. Few thought that soon there would be more people watching the television than listening to the radio.

Right: Baird was the first person to transmit an image using just the light shining on an object (rather than transmitting images of objects sending out light such as light bulbs). Using the apparatus shown here, Baird demonstrated television in 1925. The picture on Baird's 'Televisor' was made up of 30 lines and it flickered at 12½ pictures per second.

Developments in television

In 1954, the National Television System Committee (NTSC) in America had devised an ingenious way of sending information about colour. It took up no more space in the waveband than a black and white signal. It was compatible with an ordinary black and white set. However a special colour receiver could decode the colour signals and display the picture in full colour.

Many colour systems were developed based on the NTSC system. Only the French SECAM and the German PAL systems achieved any importance. Europe tried to decide upon a common system but was unable to reach a joint decision. In Britain, colour television was officially launched on 1 July 1967 with the broadcast of the Wimbledon tennis championships.

In Europe, most television systems use 625 lines. This gives a much better picture on a larger screen. Of course, more information has to be transmitted, and this means a larger bandwidth. So the 625 transmissions were established on the UHF (ultra high frequency) wavebands.

Video recording

Recording a television, or video, signal onto magnetic tape is much more difficult than recording a sound signal. There is a lot more information in a video signal and the tape would have to travel at an impossibly high speed. The problem was solved by recording the tracks across the width of the tape, instead of along the length. Video recorders have now been in use for about 25 years. Very soon after they were introduced most broadcasts started to be pre-recorded. Today there are few 'live' broadcasts.

Over the last few years domestic video cassette recorders have changed the pattern of television viewing. More and more people are buying, or borrowing pre-recorded cassette tapes and watching them on their television set.

Teletext

This is a way of sending information on the back of a television signal. With a few extra microchips in your television set you can receive up to date written information on the news, weather, sports, or the latest share prices on the Stock Exchange. It is possible to select from over 800 pages of information. If you wish you can arrange for news flashes to come up when you are watching ordinary television. For those who are hard of hearing teletext can be used to add subtitles to television programmes.

Satellite broadcasting

Satellites can relay television programmes direct to your home. Of course, you have to have a dish aerial and the right receiving equipment. Direct broadcasting by satellite (DBS) will probably be most useful to those countries without an established transmission network.

Long distance reception

There are many enthusiasts who, with very sensitive receivers, try to get pictures from as far away as possible. Reception depends upon various layers of the Earth's atmosphere. Under certain conditions, these layers can reflect the UHF signals. Sunspot activity can sometimes affect the Earth's atmosphere so that stations 19,000 km away can be received.

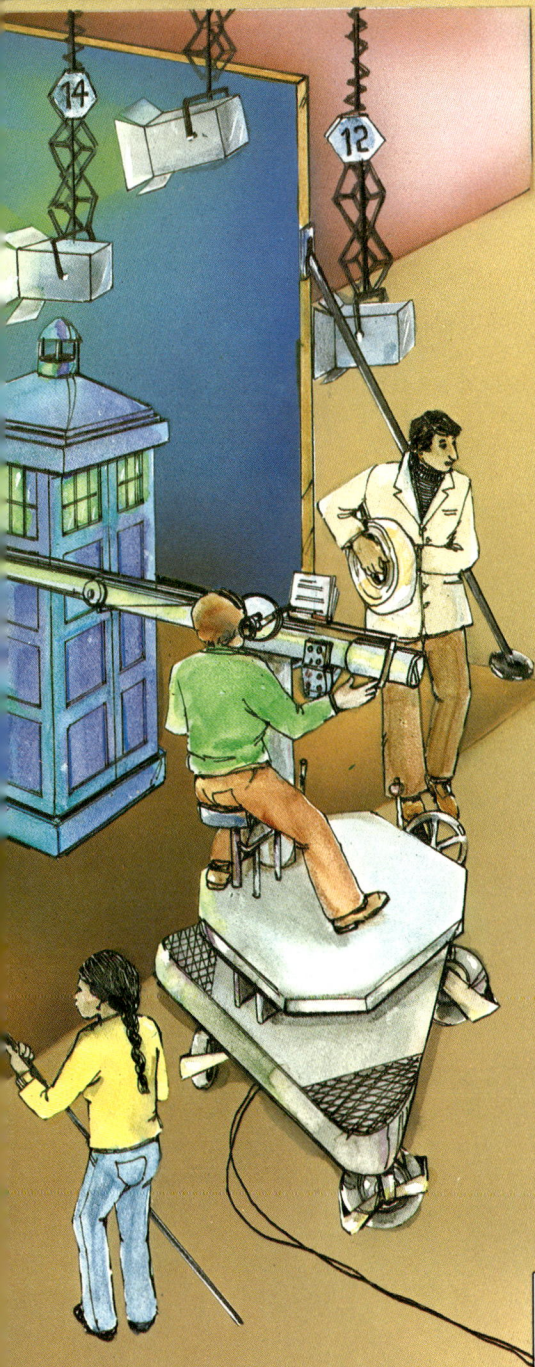

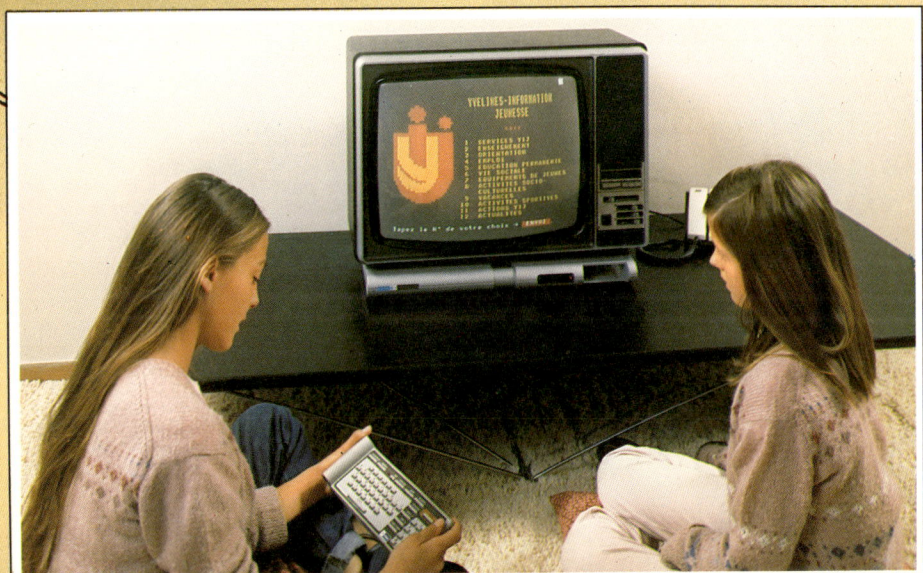

Left: Making television programmes requires teamwork. Many people are involved, from the producer to the tea-boy. Some very sophisticated, and expensive equipment is also needed.

Right: Viewdata uses a television set to display information stored on a computer. The information is not broadcast but is sent down the telephone line. This allows information to be sent in both directions. In England the system has been developed by British Telecom and is known as Prestel. Here two French girls are using the French equivalent, Télétel.

Microwave links

Microwaves are very short radio waves. The wavelength of microwaves is less than 100 cm, which means their frequency is greater than 300 MHz. As the work on radar had shown, they could be focused into a narrow beam, just as the light beam from a torch is focused by the reflector.

Line of sight
Unlike most other radio waves, microwaves are easily stopped by buildings, trees and other obstacles. Therefore the transmitting and receiving stations must be in line of sight with each other.

The aerials used to transmit microwaves are shallow dishes, about two to three metres in diameter. They focus the microwaves into very narrow beams.

Since the beams are so narrow it is unlikely that one beam will interfere with another. Also, microwaves are very economical in the energy they use. There is no need to waste energy transmitting radio waves in directions in which there are no receivers.

One of the biggest advantages of microwaves is the amount of information they can carry. There is a simple rule. The higher the frequency of the radio waves, the more information they can carry.

Microwaves have a very short wavelength and a very high frequency. Special equipment is needed for microwaves to be used for communication and this was developed from the work on radar during the Second World War.

Waveguides
Ordinary wires are not much good at carrying very high frequency electric currents. Even coaxial cables, at a frequency above about 3 GHz (3,000 MHz) do not conduct very well. The losses in the conductors and the insulator cause the signal strength to decrease greatly along the length. The answer is to use a hollow metal tube – called a waveguide. This literally 'guides' radio waves from an amplifier to a microwave aerial dish, for example.

A microwave link consists of a series of towers about 40 km apart. At the top of the tower are the aerials for receiving and transmitting the microwaves. Because microwaves can sometimes be slightly bent by the Earth's atmosphere there are usually two receiving aerials, one above the other. There is equipment inside the tower for restoring the signal to full strength before passing it on to the next tower.

Microwave links were first used to carry black and white television programmes to more people. Today they still carry many television programmes, but now in colour. Also, they carry many telephone circuits.

Each microwave link can send either one colour television signal or about 3,000 telephone calls at the same time. At the moment frequencies around 4 GHz are used to carry trunk telephone calls. Higher frequencies are used to carry television signals.

There is now a large network of microwave links. They are particularly useful for connecting remote regions to the main communications network, or for those places to which it would be difficult to lay a cable. A good example of this is the off-shore gas and oil installations in the North Sea.

Tropospheric scattering
The troposphere is the name given to the layer of the Earth's atmosphere nearest the ground. When there is a lot of water vapour in the troposphere, it is possible to send microwaves much further than normal line of sight operation. Using a powerful transmitter the microwaves

Left: The first public demonstration of microwave communication took place between Dover and Calais across the Channel on 31 March 1931. This successful experiment showed how useful radio waves with a frequency from 1,000–10,000 MHz could be. Since then, many thousands of relay stations have been built.

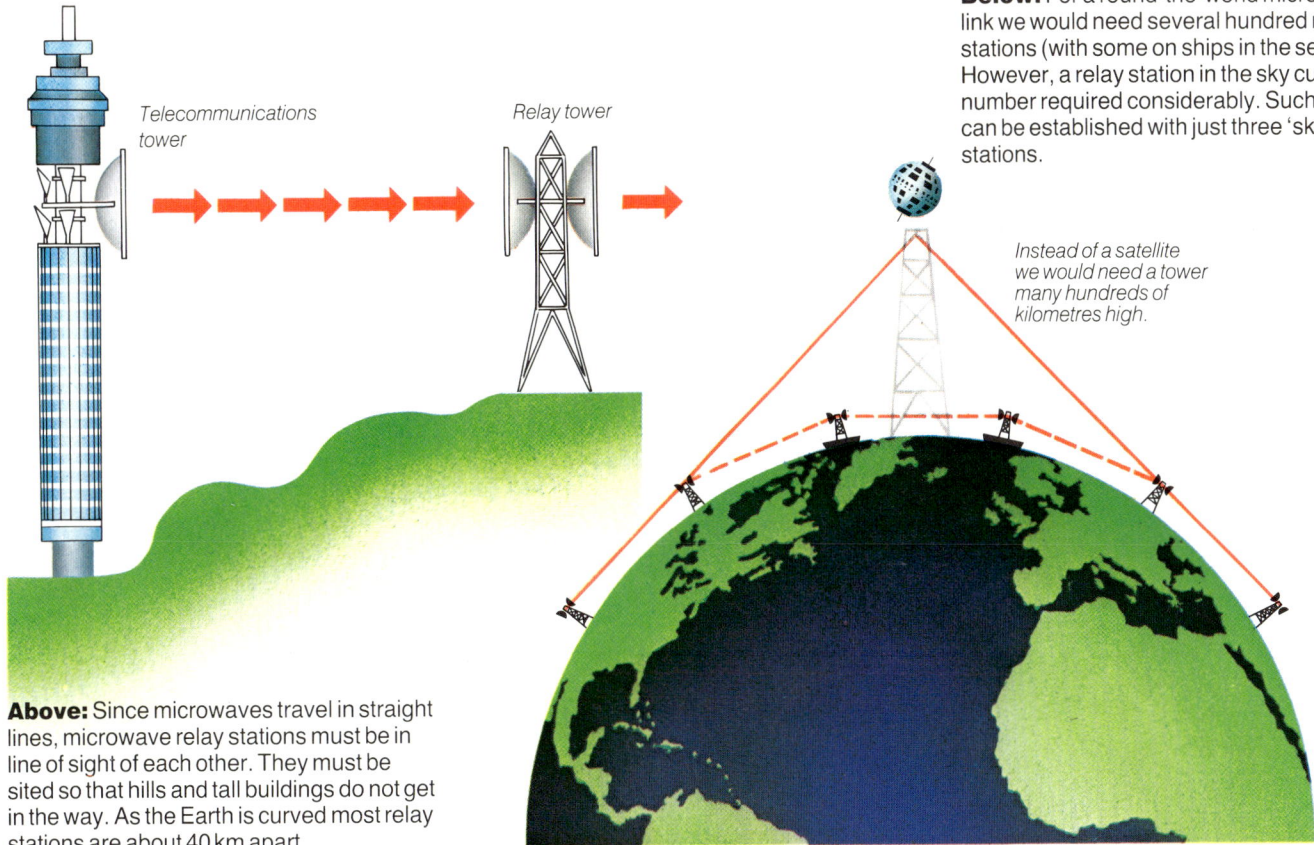

Telecommunications tower

Relay tower

Below: For a round-the-world microwave link we would need several hundred relay stations (with some on ships in the sea!). However, a relay station in the sky cuts the number required considerably. Such a link can be established with just three 'sky' stations.

Instead of a satellite we would need a tower many hundreds of kilometres high.

Above: Since microwaves travel in straight lines, microwave relay stations must be in line of sight of each other. They must be sited so that hills and tall buildings do not get in the way. As the Earth is curved most relay stations are about 40 km apart.

are 'scattered' and can be picked up over 500 km away.

This effect is used to communicate with some offshore production platforms in the North Sea gas and oil fields. Many are now 160-280 km from shore and therefore are over the horizon. Powerful transmitters and special aerials with larger billboard reflectors, 12 m or 18 m in size (see front cover), are used as the amount of scatter can vary quite considerably.

Going digital

A revolution is now taking place in how the signals are being sent. So far the information has been coded onto a carrier signal using a technique called frequency modulation. Now the information is being sent as a series of noughts and ones. These are called binary digits, or bits. As many as 280 million bits per second have been sent over a digital microwave system, and higher frequencies are still being investigated. Japan, for instance, has some local urban links which use 40 GHz.

Right: Microwave dishes are parabolic in shape. By siting the aerial feed at the focus of the reflector, a parallel beam of microwaves is sent out.

31

Satellites

A communications satellite is really a microwave relay station in space. It needs to have a very sensitive receiver because the microwaves have to travel at least 36,000 km to reach the satellite. It then re-transmits these signals, after amplifying them, back to Earth. Obviously the equipment in a satellite has to be extremely reliable.

Telstar

On 10 July 1962 Telstar was launched into a low orbit from Cape Canaveral, USA. Telstar was the world's first communications satellite. Three Earth stations had also been designed and built; Andover (Maine, USA), Pleumeur Boudou (Brittany, France) and Goonhilly Downs (Cornwall, England). The experiment showed that it was possible to telephone and to send television pictures across the Atlantic using a satellite.

Telstar circled the Earth about every two hours and was therefore only 'visible' to the aerial at Goonhilly Down for twenty minutes at a time. The satellite was moving very fast, between 17,600 and 28,000 km per hour, across the sky. It was very difficult to keep the aerial pointing at the satellite and to find it as it appeared above the horizon.

Arthur C. Clarke

In 1945, Arthur Clarke had suggested a way of using a satellite to provide a continuous link between ground stations.

The speed of any object circling the Earth depends on its distance from the Earth. The further away a satellite is from the Earth the slower it moves. Arthur Clarke worked out that there was one orbit 36,000 km above the equator in which the time the satellite takes to do one complete revolution is the same as that of the Earth. This makes it seem as if the satellite is stationary above the Earth. This is called the geostationary orbit.

Early Bird

On 6 April 1965 Early Bird was launched into a geostationary orbit. The frequency of signals sent to the satellite was 6 GHz. Early Bird picked up these signals, changed their frequency to 4 GHz, amplified them and transmitted them back down to Earth. Panels of solar cells on the outside of the satellite provided the power to do this. The power of the signal transmitted from the satellite was only 1 watt. This is extremely small – about one hundredth the power of an average light bulb.

Ground stations have to pick up a very tiny fraction of this very weak signal and amplify it without distortion or increasing the amount of noise.

Expansion

The satellite communication system has expanded rapidly. Satellite transmissions now cover the Atlantic, Pacific and Indian oceans. Demand has risen so rapidly that just six years after Early Bird was launched there were 13 satellites in geostationary orbit and over 200 Earth stations.

Each new satellite that went into orbit was bigger and better than the one before. Early Bird could handle 240 tele-

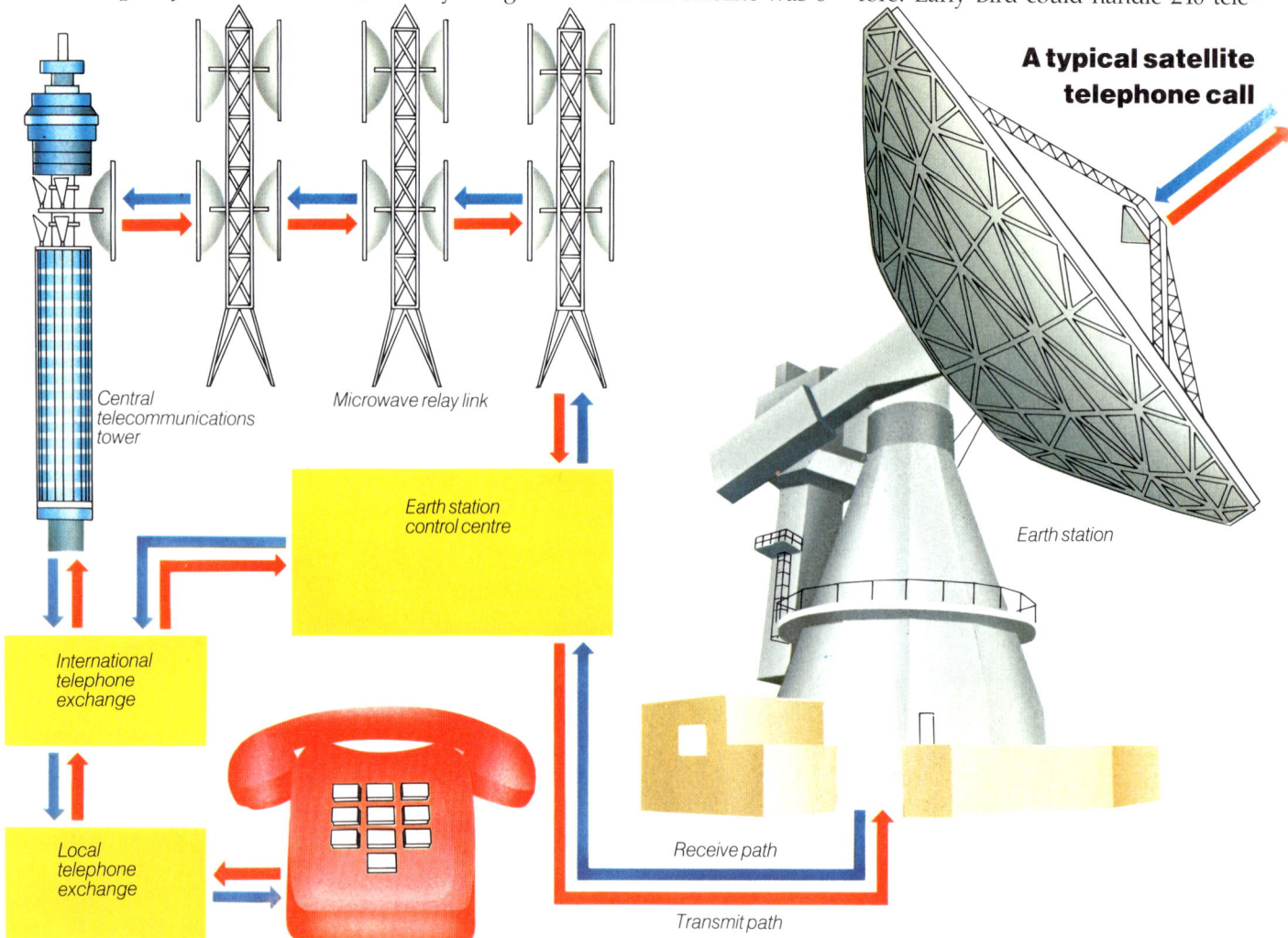

Central telecommunications tower

Microwave relay link

Earth station control centre

International telephone exchange

Local telephone exchange

A typical satellite telephone call

Earth station

Receive path

Transmit path

phone calls at once. Intelsat VI will be able to cope with 33,000 telephone calls at once. There is also a system called INMARSAT which provides a communications system for ships at sea.

INTELSAT is the name of the first international organisation which was formed to provide and manage satellites. Now over 100 countries belong to it.

European Communications Satellite

Now satellites are beginning to use digital techniques. This will increase even more the amount of information that a satellite can handle. The European Communications Satellite (ECS) system will use these digital techniques. It will provide links between the telephone networks of Europe.

Satellites handle telephone calls, telex messages, computer data, electronic mail and document facsimiles. Today satellites offer a cheap service, especially to Third World countries with no established cable system.

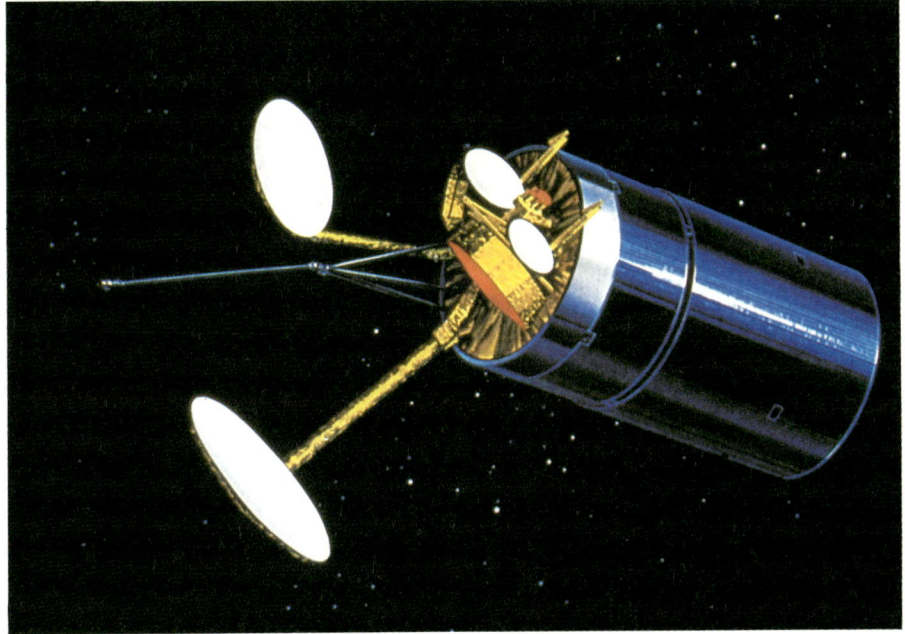

Above: Modern rockets can now put communication satellites, such as the Intelsat series, weighing nearly 2,000 kg into geostationary orbit.

Below: Earth stations are big so they can pick up the very weak signals coming from satellites and spacecraft, and accurately beam powerful signals to them.

Exploring space

July 1969 was memorable since not only was a man walking on the Moon, but millions of people on Earth could watch it as it happened.

Nations all over the world co-operated to bring the pictures to as many people as possible. It was rather complicated. The Earth rotates on its axis and only part of the world can 'see' the Moon at any one time. So Earth stations took it in turn to receive the signals and pass them on to everyone else.

Sputnik

The space age began when the USSR launched Sputnik in 1957. Many enthusiasts listened on their short-wave radios as Sputnik bleeped its way round the Earth.

Astronomers first explored space by just looking and observing very carefully. Telescopes made this easier and also enabled them to see a lot more. But our eyes can only see a very small part of the radiation in the electromagnetic spectrum. In the 1930s radio telescopes were first used. They showed that weak radio signals were coming from the Milky Way, Venus and Jupiter.

Robot explorers

It was thought that the best explorer of space would be a person. However, it is very expensive to send people into space. Robots are much cheaper, and they don't mind a one-way trip. So many unmanned robot spacecraft have been sent off to explore the other planets in our solar system.

Robot spacecraft visited Mars and sent back pictures which disappointed many people on Earth. They showed Mars to be a cold planet with enormous dust storms raging over the surface. Even Venus, once thought to be rather like Earth, was shown to be extremely hot, with acid rain.

Voyagers 1 and 2 have both sent back pictures and details of Jupiter and Saturn. Some instruments have been shut down, but others will continue to send back information as the spacecraft head towards the far reaches of the solar system.

Voyager 2 still has two missions to accomplish. It is now heading towards Uranus which it will reach in January 1986. Three years later it will pass Neptune, 12 years after leaving Earth. Voyager 2 will become the spacecraft furthest

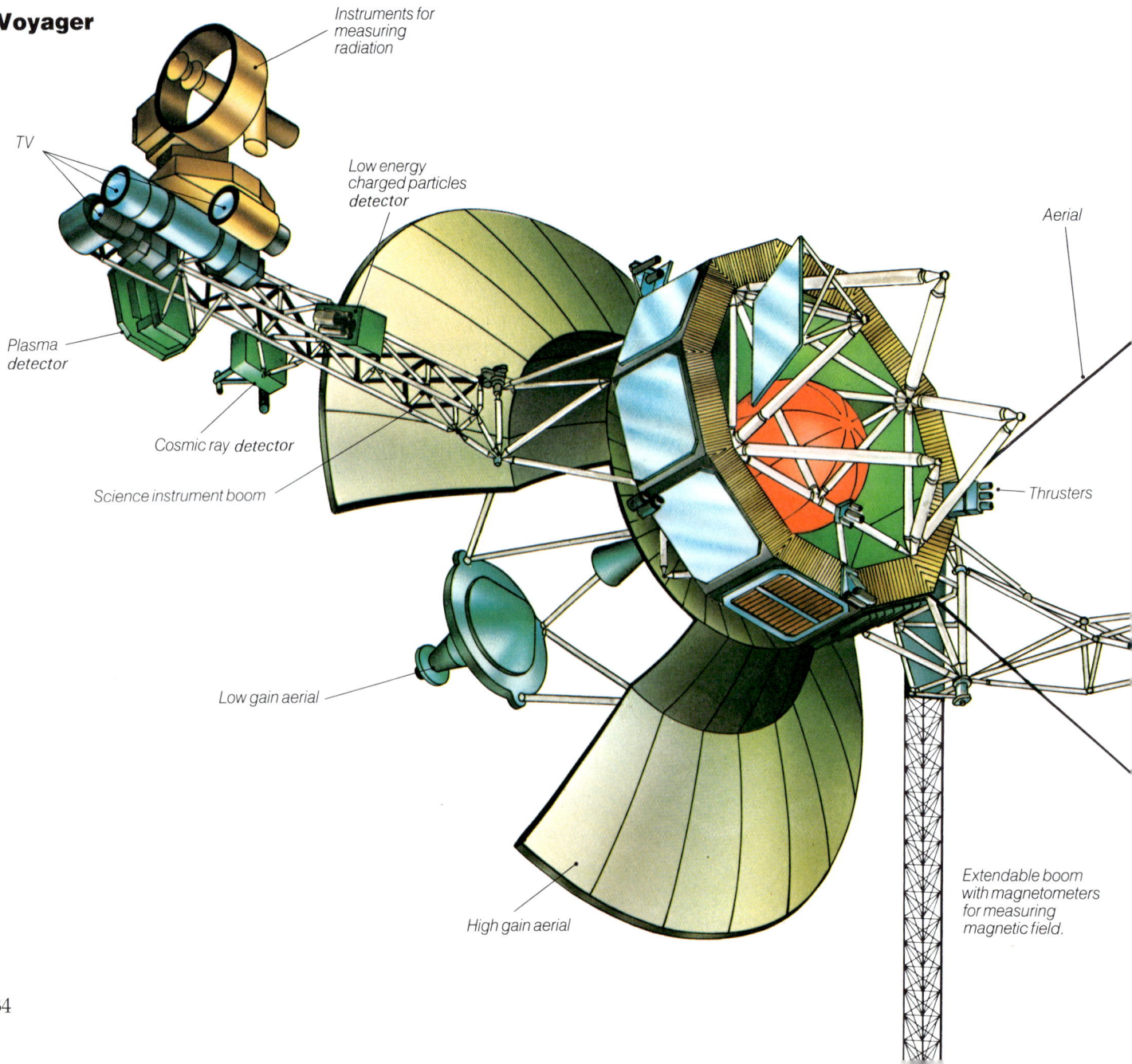

Voyager

Instruments for measuring radiation

TV

Low energy charged particles detector

Plasma detector

Cosmic ray *detector*

Science instrument boom

Low gain aerial

High gain aerial

Aerial

Thrusters

Extendable boom with magnetometers for measuring magnetic field.

away from us with which we can communicate.

Voyager's power output is about a fifth of the power of an average light bulb. Only one millionth, millionth, millionth part of these waves reaches Earth. Receiving these signals is like trying to see a glow-worm from a distance of many thousand miles.

In 1964 Mariner 4 took nine days to send 22 pictures of Mars back to Earth. Over the next 16 years communication techniques improved so much that Voyager was able to send a picture every 48 seconds.

Below: The two Voyager spacecraft carry a variety of complex scientific equipment and experiments for trying to discover more about space and other planets.

Generators

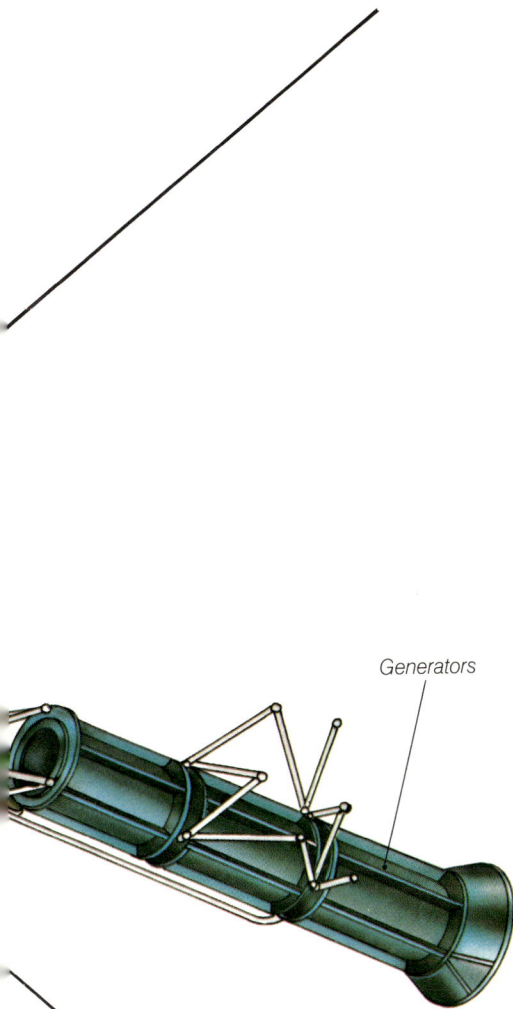

Above: Voyager 2 took this picture of Saturn on 12 July 1981. The pictures which the Voyager spacecraft sent back revealed the presence of several new moons.

Below: There are many different types of satellite in orbit. METEOSAT, a satellite for weather forecasters, took this picture of Africa.

Technical aspects

Radar

Visible light

X-rays

Ultra-violet

10^{20}

Infra-red

Radio waves

10^1

The part of the spectrum available for communication ranges from 10^4 Hz to over 10^{14} Hz.

10^{14}

10^{13}

10^{12}

10^{11}

10^{10}

Frequency in Hertz

10^9

10^8

10^7

10^6

10^5

10^4

Fibre optic communications

Microwave communications

Medium wave radio

Black and white TV

Colour TV

These coloured bands show how more space (or bandwidth) is available at higher frequencies.

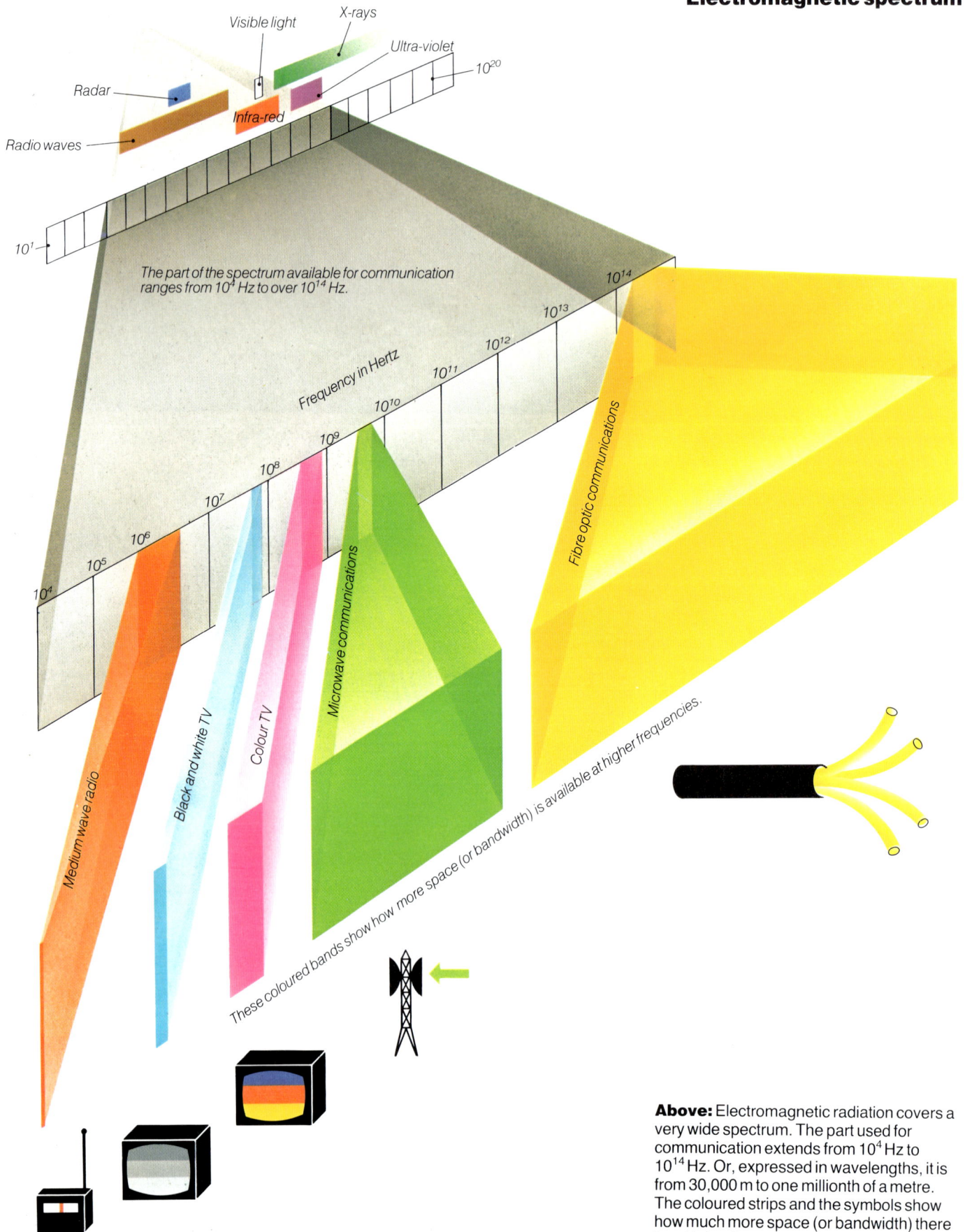

Above: Electromagnetic radiation covers a very wide spectrum. The part used for communication extends from 10^4 Hz to 10^{14} Hz. Or, expressed in wavelengths, it is from 30,000 m to one millionth of a metre. The coloured strips and the symbols show how much more space (or bandwidth) there is at higher frequencies.

It is now easy to telephone someone on the other side of the world. But it is rather hard to understand why it is so easy. It all seems very complicated and there are lots of long words – even the word telecommunications itself! Some people do not even bother to use words, they just use groups of letters. You hear and read, STD, PCM, TDM, AM and FM. What do they all mean?

You will find what these groups of letters, and others, stand for in the glossary. But learning what the letters stand for is only the beginning. On these pages some of the technical aspects which are common to all kinds of communication systems are explained.

Electromagnetic spectrum

Light waves, radio waves, x-rays and cosmic rays are all connected. They are part of the electromagnetic spectrum. They all travel at the speed of light, which is 300,000,000 metres per second. Waves in this spectrum obey the simple rule:

wavelength × frequency = speed of light.

Unfortunately, people are not consistent. Sometimes we describe radio waves by their frequency and at other times by their wavelength. There is a table in the reference section which gives the frequency and wavelength of radio waves in each frequency band.

Bandwidth

This describes the amount of space or range of frequency that is needed to send various types of information.

If speech is sent through the telephone then frequencies up to 4000 kHz must be transmitted. Another way of putting this is to say that the bandwidth needed for a telephone channel is 4 kHz.

A colour television signal however needs a much larger bandwidth of 8 MHz, 2,000 times bigger. But a telex only needs 1/20th of the bandwidth required for one telephone channel.

Now the HF (high frequency) band covers frequencies from 3 MHz to 30 MHz, which is a range of 27 MHz. So three television signals would practically fill it up! Alternatively there is room for 6750 telephone channels.

Pulse code modulation (PCM)

PCM is a digital way of sending information using just numbers. First the signal is sampled by measuring the amplitude of the signal every 1/8000th of a second. This amplitude is then quantized, or turned into a number between 0 and 255. This number is then converted into binary and sent as a series of pulses to the receiver. The receiver has to reverse the process and put the signal back together again.

It is possible to send several signals at

Above: A Ferranti microchip just a few millimetres square turns speech into numbers, turning into reality the dream of PCM that Alex Reeves had in 1937.

once along one line using PCM by a technique called Time Division Multiplexing (TDM). As a signal is only sampled very quickly every 1/8000th of a second there is time to sample other signals whilst waiting for the next 1/8000th of a second to come along. All the signals can then be sent as a stream of numbers in exactly the same way as for PCM.

Below: Pulse Code Modulation and Time Division Multiplexing.

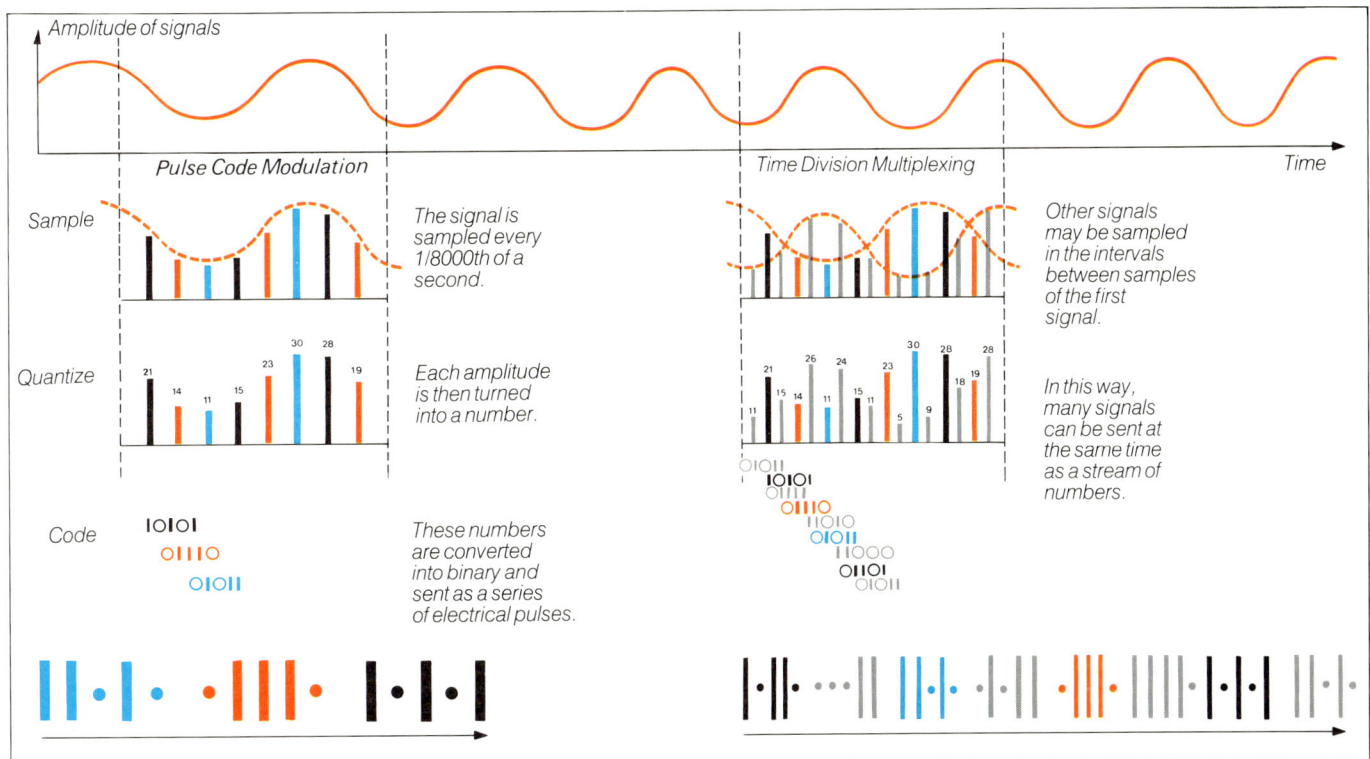

37

Optical fibres and lasers

Light was one of the first means of communication we used. Messages were sent using beacons of fire. In the 18th century Chappe devised his semaphore telegraph system. It depended on light. The big problem with using light is that bad weather, such as rain, mist and fog, can prevent us seeing far. So for the last one hundred and fifty years we have communicated using pulses of electricity along wires or with radio waves. Now, due to some recent inventions, we are returning to light.

Right: Optical fibres may look attractive, but they are very difficult to make!

Below: There are several ways in which a thin strand of glass can conduct light. One way is to make the strand so thin that the light has to go straight along it ('monomode'). It is very difficult to make strands of glass such as these so it was soon found that thicker strands of glass could also conduct light by reflecting it off the boundary between two different types of glass, with different refractive indices ('multimode'). The latest type of optical fibre has glass in the centre with a high index which gradually decreases towards the outside.

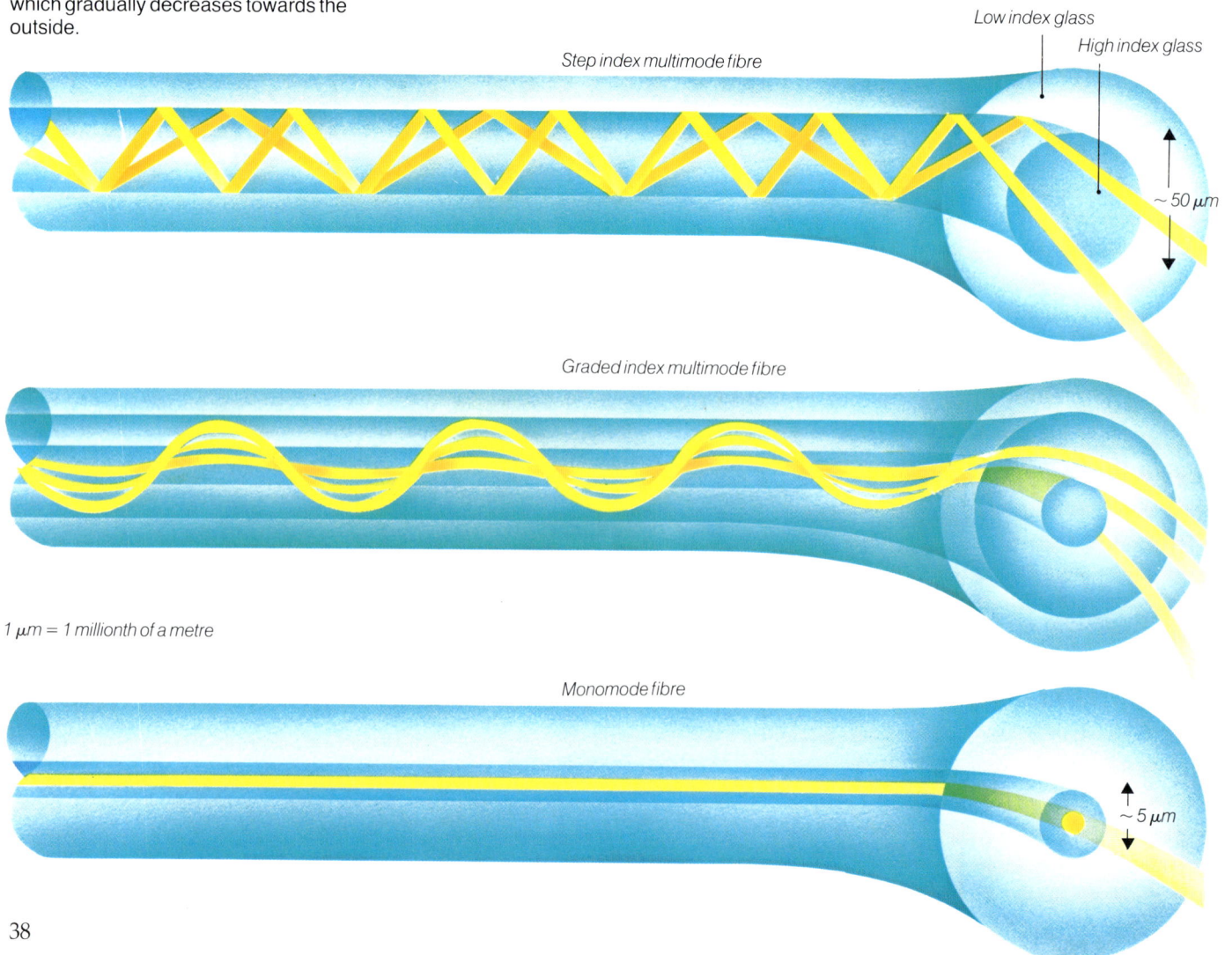

Step index multimode fibre

Low index glass

High index glass

~50 μm

Graded index multimode fibre

1 μm = 1 millionth of a metre

Monomode fibre

~5 μm

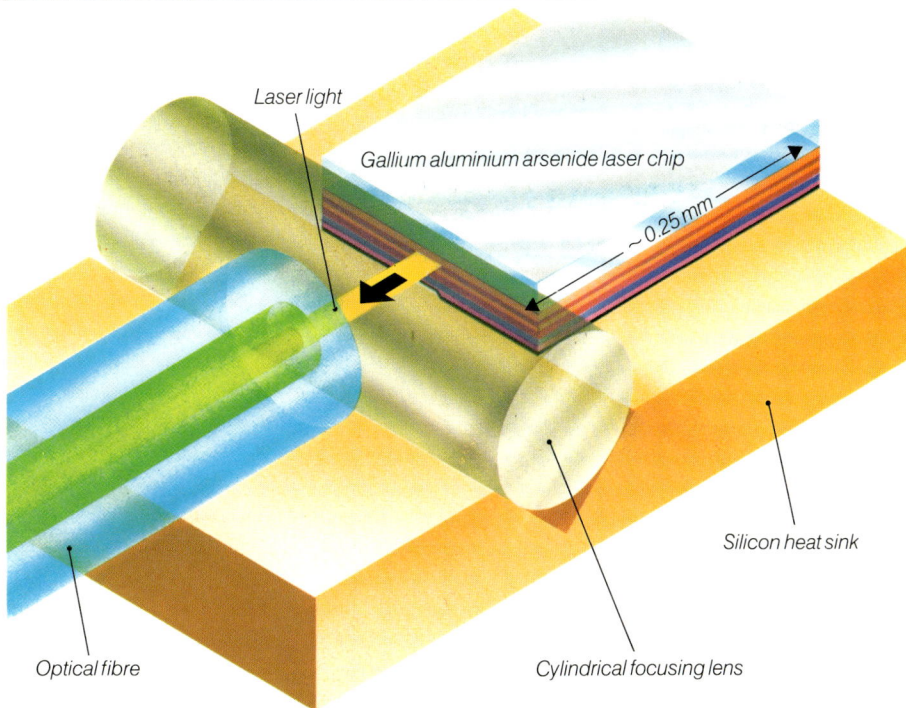

Laser light

Gallium aluminium arsenide laser chip

~ 0.25 mm

Silicon heat sink

Cylindrical focusing lens

Optical fibre

Above: Thin layers of atoms are 'laid' on top of the base material (such as gallium arsenide) to build up a solid-state laser. The layer which sends out the laser beam is less than a millionth of a metre thick.

Below: This photograph gives an idea of the size of each optical fibre. Many can pass through the eye of a needle. The fibre with a green light coming out of it is a 'multimode' one. The other is a 'monomode' fibre.

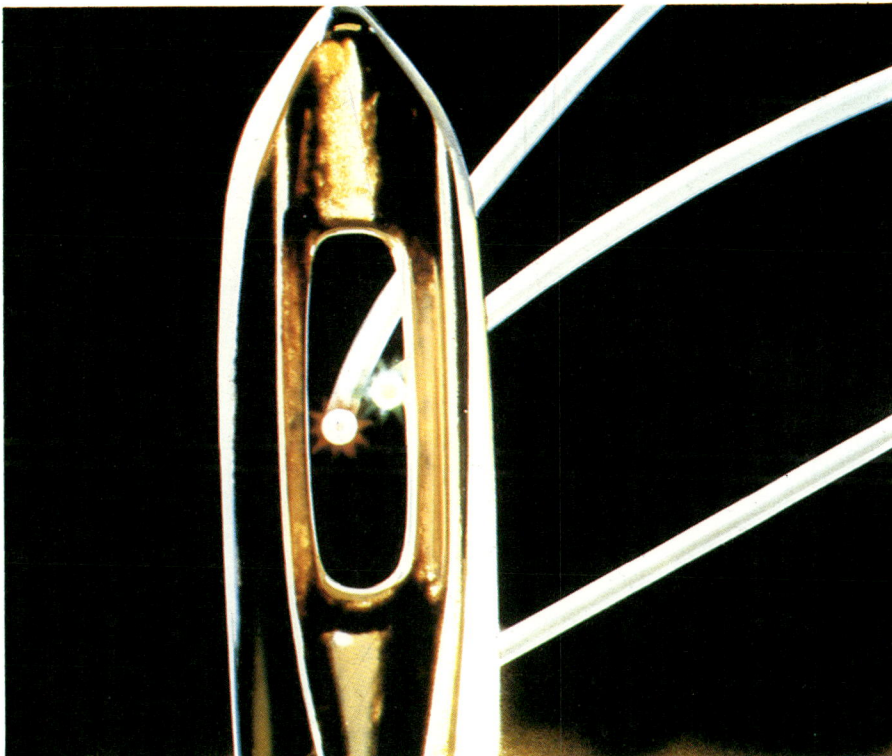

Glass conductors

Light is easily stopped by particles in the air such as rain and dust. We need to find a way of 'conducting' light over long distances reliably and efficiently.

Cat's-eyes appear to glow as a car approaches with its lights on. This is because the pieces of glass in the cat's-eyes send the light from the headlights back to the car. This is by total internal reflection inside the pieces of glass. The conducting of light down an optical fibre works on the same principle.

In 1966 Kao and Hockham, working at STC's research laboratories, suggested using a tiny strand of glass to conduct pulses of light. The glass has to be very pure, purer than ordinary glass. This has impurities in it which scatter the light. Try looking end-on at a pane of glass – it appears green. Special glass called sodium borosilicate has to be used. You would be able to see through a block of this glass several kilometres thick.

Pulses of light

The little pulses of light are produced by recently invented semiconductor devices. They are the only devices capable of switching on and off fast enough. One device is the LED (light emitting diode). These produce the familiar little red lights in some calculators and other electronic equipment. The other device is the semiconductor laser. A laser produces a pulse of light which is all at the same frequency. LEDs, however, produce light which has a broad range of frequencies.

It is rather misleading to call them pulses of 'light' as the ones which are used in optical fibre communication cannot be seen by the human eye! The special glass is more transparent to light in the infra-red part of the spectrum. Our eyes are not sensitive to light in this frequency range.

Since LEDs and lasers can only switch on and off, pulse code modulation (see page 37) must be used. Everything must be changed into little "bits" of information. Now since the frequency of light is so high, the bandwidth of the optical fibre, or the amount of information that can be carried, is very large. It has the potential to carry 100,000 times more than a coaxial cable.

The optical fibre cables are smaller and lighter and need fewer repeaters on long distances. Also, they are not affected by electrical interference.

In busy cities cables are laid in underground ducts. These ducts are now full. The smaller fibre optic cables will replace the old copper ones and there will still be lots of room for expansion.

One optical fibre cable into your home will be able to carry many services at the same time. You could have several television programmes to watch, use a video telephone, send or receive computer data, or look to see if you had any electronic mail.

Computers take control

Above: This computer communication system gives international currency dealers up to the minute details of changes in the world's foreign exchange markets.

Below: Earth stations need computer-controlled systems to keep the massive aerials pointing towards the satellites. This computer room is at Goonhilly Downs.

As computers developed and began to be used more widely in commerce and industry, it soon became clear that it would be useful for them to communicate with each other. For instance, suppose computer A has a list of names and addresses in its memory. Computer B, a long way away, would like to use them. It is rather silly for A to print them out and for someone then to type them into B. The more efficient way is for A to talk to B directly.

Twenty years ago computers started to use ordinary telegraph and telephone lines to talk to one another. A special piece of equipment, called a modem, is needed to convert the computer signals into a form that can be sent over a telephone line.

A little crackle on a telephone line does not prevent you from understanding what the other person is saying. But it could have disastrous results for a computer. So special lines were brought into use which were more reliable and capable of taking more information than the public telephone network.

Computers work using just 0s and 1s as the electronic circuits in them have two states: off and on. A 0 or a 1 is called a binary digit, or a bit of information. The speed of a system is given by how many bits of information it can transfer every second.

High speed computers can turn speech, television pictures, music, photographs and computer data into a stream of bits.

Those bits can either be represented as pulses of electricity or as little flashes of light. Since the information is in bits it is easy to send it anywhere in seconds.

The information can be sent along conventional cables, coaxial cables, optical fibres, microwave radio links and satellites. Even a telephone call will probably be sent using several different methods. Computers have to control the routeing of all the bits of information. They have to make sure that each bit ends up at its correct destination and that the information is re-assembled correctly.

Packet switching

When you make a telephone call the exchange switches you through to the person you want to speak to. There is a wire connecting you. Of course, no-one else can use the line, to ring you up for instance – you are engaged. All this is very wasteful of time and also expensive. It is rather like everyone having

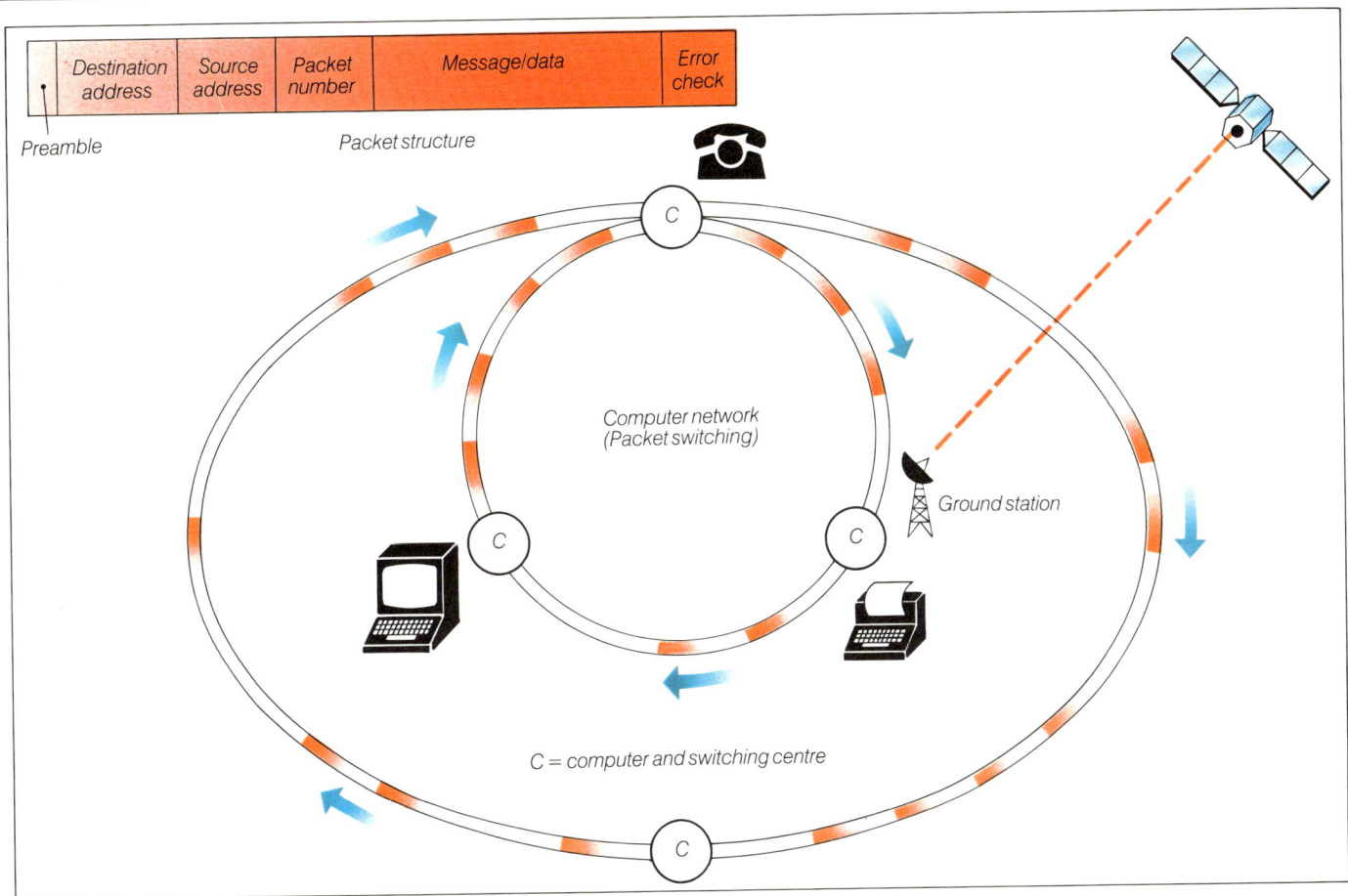

Preamble	Destination address	Source address	Packet number	Message/data	Error check

Packet structure

Computer network
(Packet switching)

Ground station

C = computer and switching centre

their own private road to get to school or work. Sharing roads with many others is sensible. Now a similar thing is happening with computer networks. Computers, and other machines, share the lines joining them together.

The 'links' can be ordinary telephone wires, coaxial cables, optical fibres, or satellites. There have to be 'switching centres' which control which bit goes where. Very fast computers are needed for this.

Short messages are sent with a label on them stating their destination. Also there is error checking. This checks to see if a mistake has been made sending the message. If it has, the receiver asks for the message to be corrected and sent again. The switching centres send the messages by the quickest possible route to their destination.

Long messages are best split up into packets. Each packet is sent separately. So parts of a long message may end up going via several different routes. At each stage the packets are checked for errors in transmission. If any are found, the packet is sent again. The packets are numbered so that they can be put back in the correct order when they have all arrived safely.

Above: Packet switching is used for sending large messages long distances. The message is split up into small packets which are sent by different routes.

Below: Local Area Networks (LAN) pass messages between computers. It is like a continuous train: messages are put in the first empty wagon passing the sender.

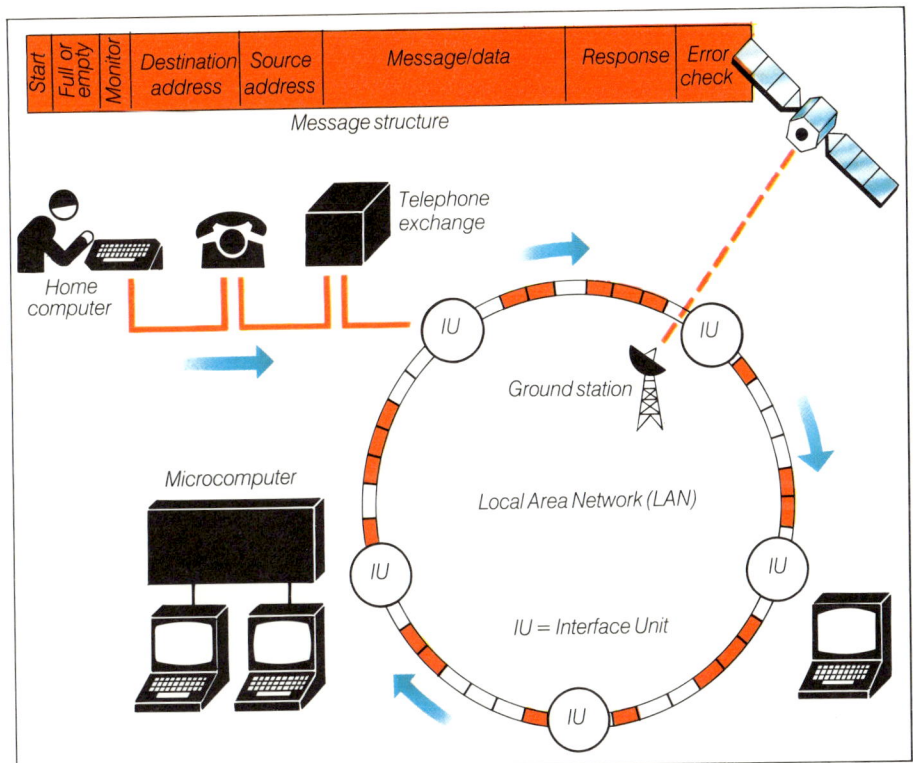

Start	Full or empty	Monitor	Destination address	Source address	Message/data	Response	Error check

Message structure

Home computer

Telephone exchange

Ground station

Microcomputer

Local Area Network (LAN)

IU = Interface Unit

Shape of things to come

We have seen how telecommunications have grown over the last 200 years. The effects on our lives have been enormous. Imagine bringing someone who lived 200 years ago into today's world and showing them the telephone, radio, television, satellites, pictures of Venus, optical fibres and so on. They would probably be overwhelmed and suspect it was all done by magic.

In the last 25 years we have seen the development of satellites, optical fibres and digital techniques. What major inventions and discoveries will be made in the next 25 years? This question is impossible to answer. We can only speculate about what may happen over the next few years with existing technologies.

Today many people are overwhelmed by the increasing speed at which new developments are taking place. One hundred years ago there seemed to be more time between inventions. People had time to get used to the electric telegraph before the telephone appeared. Now inventions and improvements take place so rapidly that it is difficult to even keep track of what is happening.

The ability to send and receive all kinds of information, whether words, pictures or computer data to the other side of the world almost instantaneously is still new.

We have not explored all the possible uses of these techniques. Also, what effect will they have on our lives?

Satellites will be larger and handle more information. The Space Shuttle will be able to take them into space, rather than using expensive use-once-

only rockets. Perhaps it may be economic to service satellites in orbit, or to bring them back to earth for repair.

Experiments with broadcasting by satellite will continue and some large businesses will have their own small Earth station to send and receive data at very high speeds.

The trends in micro-electronics seem likely to continue. Components will continue to become cheaper, smaller and faster.

Sending messages in 'bits' has only just begun. Many links will convert from analogue methods to digital ones capable of sending all kinds of information.

Optical fibres look promising. They can carry a lot more information than conventional cables. They are also smaller. Schemes are being suggested for connecting all homes together with optical fibres. Then we should be able to choose between many more television programmes, to shop from the comfort of our armchairs, and to send and receive mail just by using our own computer terminal.

Even now it is possible using a home computer and the telephone system to dial into several large computer systems in other countries. The main problem is security. How do you keep your personal information to yourself and stop other people looking at it or using the money in your bank account?

Exploring space continues and new stars are being discovered. The space telescope will certainly reveal many new interesting facts about the universe. Exploring space and the world around us may not only reveal details of the world we live in but may also tell us more about ourselves.

In the 1930s, H. G. Wells said that telecommunications was 'abolishing distance – heedlessly and recklessly'. It is true that telecommunications is abolishing distance and making the world a smaller place. Primitive people lived in their small community and worked and fought for its survival. The community we live in is the whole world. Now it is up to us to share resources and information to ensure the survival of our community – the world.

Right: Ariane, the rocket developed by the European Space Agency, is used to put communication satellites into orbit.

Left: The space telescope will become the largest astronomical telescope operating outside the blanketing effect of the Earth's atmosphere.

A-Z Glossary

Aerial (or antenna) A wire, rod or dish to send and receive radio waves.

Amplifier A device which increases the strength of an electrical signal by electronic circuits using valves, transistors or microchips.

Amplitude The height or range of vibration of a wave.

Amplitude Modulation (AM) A way of varying the amplitude of a wave to carry information.

Analogue A signal in which the amplitude, or frequency, of the signal directly represents the original signal, such as the output from a microphone.

Bandwidth The amount of space or range of frequencies in the electromagnetic spectrum occupied by a signal, (about 10 kHz for a radio signal and about 4 MHz for a TV signal).

Binary A means of counting using only 0's and 1's.

Bit An abbreviation of **b**inary dig**it**: either a 0 or 1.

Bits Per Second (BPS) The number of bits sent per second by a data communications system.

Carrier The wave on which information is superimposed by modulation.

Cathode-Ray Tube (CRT) A high-vacuum tube in which a beam of electrons from the cathode (negative terminal) hits a screen which glows where the beam hits it. There is one in every television set.

Coaxial cable A cable with a central conductor within an outer tubular conductor with an insulator between e.g. TV aerial cable.

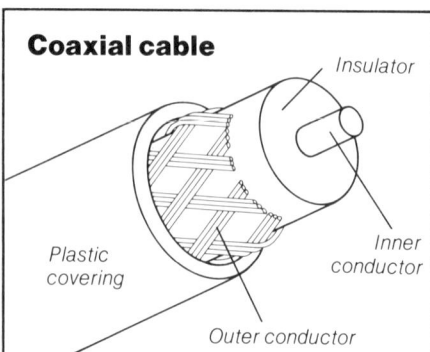

Coaxial cable

Insulator

Plastic covering

Inner conductor

Outer conductor

Data Words, numbers or other symbols which communication systems send and receive.

Detector The part of a receiver in which the information is extracted from the modulated signal received.

Digital transmissions Those which use only numbers (in the form of bits) whether as data or to represent for instance a sound signal. They are preferred because of their accuracy and are taking over from the traditional analogue system.

Dish A reflector which focuses a beam of waves.

Duct A tube along which cables are laid.

Electromagnetic spectrum The whole range of waves, such as radio and light waves, which are made up of the combined fluctuations of electric and magnetic fields.

Electromagnetism Magnetism produced by an electrical current.

Exchange A central place where telephone connections are made.

Frequency The number of waves per second, measured in Hertz.

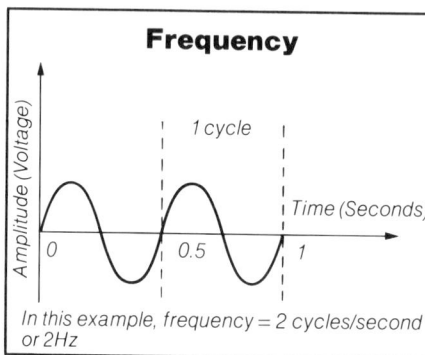

Frequency

Amplitude (Voltage)

1 cycle

Time (Seconds)

0   0.5   1

In this example, frequency = 2 cycles/second or 2Hz

Frequency Division Multiplexing (FDM) A way of sending more than one signal at once by modulating each signal onto a different carrier wave. This is an analogue method of transmission often used in microwave links.

Frequency Modulation (FM) A way of varying the frequency of a wave to carry information.

Gigahertz (GHz) See Hertz.

Hertz A measure of frequency of radio waves; 1 Hertz = 1 vibration per second, 1 kilohertz (kHz) = 1,000 Hertz, 1 megahertz (MHz) = 1,000,000 Hertz, 1 gigahertz (GHz) = 1,000,000,000 Hertz.

Interference A crackling noise which can be caused for instance by thunder-storms, or by electric motors and car ignition systems. Another type of interference makes the received signal fade.

Ionosphere The upper part of the Earth's atmosphere consisting of several layers which can reflect radio waves. The layers are electrically conducting because they contain charged particles.

Kilohertz (kHz) See Hertz.

Laser A device which gives a pure and concentrated light beam. The letters stand for Light Amplification by Stimulated Emission of Radiation.

Link A communication path between two points in both directions. It consists of two channels, one in each direction.

Loss The decrease in the power of a transmitted signal along a cable.

Loudspeaker an electromagnetic mechanism which produces sound waves, e.g. in radio and TV sets.

Megahertz (MHz) See Hertz.

Microphone A device for converting sound waves into electricity.

Microwaves Extremely high frequency radio waves (about 1,000 MHz to 1,000,000 MHz) used to carry information. (Microwave ovens use these waves to heat food.)

Modem A device that converts computer data into a form that can be sent over an ordinary telephone line and makes incoming signals intelligible to a computer.

Modulation The process of putting information onto a carrier wave.

Morse Code A signalling system which uses various combinations of dots and dashes to represent letters of the alphabet and numbers.

Multiplexing A way of sending many messages at the same time through one wire.

Noise Any unwanted disturbance that interferes with the transmitted signal.

Optical fibre A tiny flexible thread of glass which conducts laser light.

Packet switching A method of sending information from one place to another by splitting it into little packets of information which are transmitted as quickly as possible when there is time and space in the network. This is in contrast to the Public Switched Telephone Network (PSTN), in which data and speech pass continuously from sender to receiver.

Public Switched Telephone Network (PSTN) The normal telephone network which can be also used to send computer data, as well as speech.

Pulse Code Modulation (PCM) A way of converting a signal into numbers (i.e. into digital form) and sending the signal as a series of numbers. This reduces the effect of interference.

Radar A means of locating objects by reflecting radio waves off them.

Radio waves Electromagnetic waves within the radio frequencies of the electromagnetic spectrum i.e. between 10^4Hz and 10^{14}Hz. This means they range in wavelength from 30,000 m to one millionth of a metre.

Repeater An amplifier which picks up a weak signal coming along a line and sends out a new identical signal at full strength.

Satellite A vehicle sent up to orbit the Earth or other planet. Geostationary satellites are used in communications to relay radio or television signals.

Semaphore A signalling system using flags, or movable arms attached to a post, with each position representing a letter of the alphabet or a number.

Short waves Radio waves with a wavelength of about 50 m or less.

Signal Words, codes or sounds transmitted in some way.

Strowger The first electromechanical system of switching telephone circuits.

Subscriber Trunk Dialling (STD) A dialling system which allows any subscriber to dial directly to any exchange in the country, and many abroad.

Switchboard A manual device for connecting telephone users.

Telegraph A device for sending messages electrically.

Teleprinter An electromechanical machine which prints out the telegraph messages it receives.

Teletex A faster and more sophisticated form of telex, linking word processors.

Teletext A system of broadcasting information on TV channels for display on special television receivers, e.g. CEEFAX (BBC) and ORACLE (ITV).

Telex The international network of teleprinters.

Time Division Multiplexing (TDM) Sending more than one signal over the same line by slotting parts of each signal one after the other.

Total internal reflection The mechanism by which light is 'trappped' in an optical fibre. Light travelling in glass can be totally reflected back into the glass from the inside surface, if it hits it at the correct angle.

Transmit To send a message using sound or visual means; an electrical or radio signal often carries the message.

VHF Radio waves with a Very High

Total internal reflection

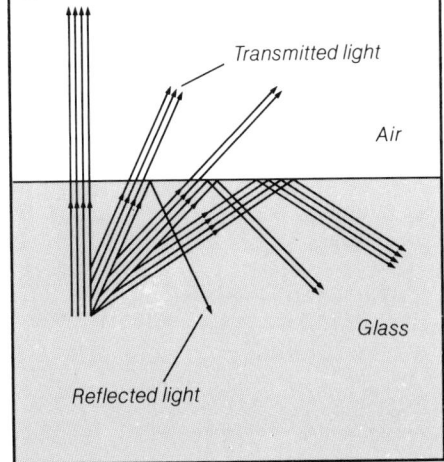

As the angle becomes bigger, more and more light is reflected on the surface between glass and air.

Frequency between 30 MHz and 300 MHz. They are used in radio communication over short distances and in high quality radio broadcasts.

Viewdata A network which can link a telephone subscriber into a central computer.

Vibration The rapid movement backwards and forwards of a sound wave or the electric and magnetic variations in a radio wave.

Waveband The range of frequencies which each radio or television channel uses. There may be room for hundreds of channels in each waveband.

Wavelength The distance between the crest on one wave and the next; in radio and television each station sends out signals at its own wavelength. A radio wavelength is usually measured in metres.

Wireless A wire-less form of communication; another name for radio.

RADIO WAVEBANDS

FREQUENCY	WAVELENGTH	NAME	TRANSMITTED BY	USED FOR
10^{14}-10^{16}Hz	3.10^{-4}-3.10^{-6}cm	Ultraviolet visible infrared	Optical fibres, lasers	Data links
30-300GHz	10-1mm	EHF (Extremely High Frequency)	Waveguides, microwave radio	Radio astronomy, radar, space communications, microwave links
3-30GHZ	10-1cm	SHF (Super High Frequency)	Waveguides, microwave radio	Radar, satellite and space communications, microwave links
300MHz-3GHz	100-10cm	UHF (Ultra High Frequency)	Shortwave radio, waveguides	UHF television, CB radio, radar, line-of-sight radio, communications (military)
30-300MHz	10-1m	VHF (Very High Frequency)	Coaxial cable, shortwave radio	VHF television, FM radio, navigational aids
3-30MHz	100-10m	HF (High Frequency)	Coaxial cable, shortwave radio	Amateur radio, mobile radio telephone, military communications, CB radio (GB)
300 kHz-3MHz	1000-100m	MF (Medium Frequency)	Coaxial cable, longwave radio	AM broadcasting, amateur radio
30-300 kHz	10^4-10^3m	LF (Low Frequency)	Wire pairs, longwave radio	Navigational aids, radio beacons, standard tone and frequency broadcasts
3Hz-30 kHz	10^8-10^4m	VLF (Very Low Frequency)	Wire pairs, longwave radio	Audio, telephone, data links, long range navigation

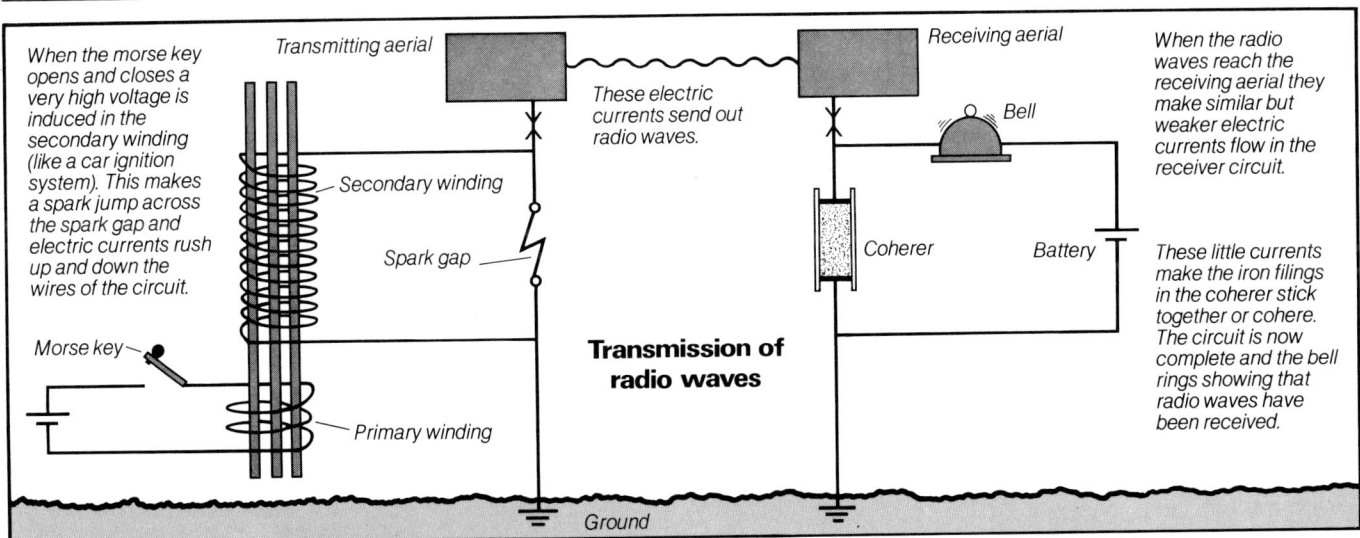

When the morse key opens and closes a very high voltage is induced in the secondary winding (like a car ignition system). This makes a spark jump across the spark gap and electric currents rush up and down the wires of the circuit.

Morse key

Transmitting aerial

Secondary winding

Spark gap

Primary winding

These electric currents send out radio waves.

Receiving aerial

Bell

Coherer

Battery

Transmission of radio waves

When the radio waves reach the receiving aerial they make similar but weaker electric currents flow in the receiver circuit.

These little currents make the iron filings in the coherer stick together or cohere. The circuit is now complete and the bell rings showing that radio waves have been received.

Ground

Reference

People and events

The following are some of the important dates connected with our understanding and use of telecommunications.

1774 Georges Lesage of Geneva built a telegraph using an electrostatic machine.

1794 Chappe completed the first mechanical semaphore telegraph, linking Paris and Lille.

1800 Volta invented the battery, the first steady source of electricity.

1820 Oersted showed that an electric current flowing in a wire could deflect a magnetic needle nearby.

1831 Faraday worked out the laws of electromagnetic effects.

1832 Schilling used the deflection of a magnetic needle to show the possibilities of the electric telegraph.

1837 Cooke and Wheatstone demonstrated the first practical electric telegraph to the directors of the newly-built London and Birmingham Railway.

1845 The first telegraph line in the USA, built by Samuel Morse, opened between Washington and Baltimore.

1850 The first submarine cable laid between England and France.

1864 Maxwell predicted the existence of radio waves.

1866 The first successful Atlantic submarine cable.

1876 Bell beat Elisha Gray to the Patent Office with his invention of the telephone.

1887 Hertz demonstrated that radio waves exist.

1891 Strowger patented his invention of an automatic telephone exchange.

1892 The first automatic telephone exchange opened at La Porte, Indiana.

1901 Marconi transmitted a message across the Atlantic using radio waves.

1903 The thermionic valve was invented by J. A. Fleming.

1906 R. A. Fessenden showed that it was possible to transmit music using radio waves.

1922 The British Broadcasting Company formed.

1925 John Logie Baird demonstrates the first television system in London.

1927 Radio-telephone service established between the UK and the USA.

1931 Experimental microwave link established across the English Channel.

1931 Karl Jansky discovered that radio waves were coming from the Milky Way and started radio astronomy.

1936 The world's first television service starts in the UK.

1937 Alec Reeves proposed Pulse Code Modulation to improve long distance speech communication.

1938 Coaxial cables first used.

1939–1945 Many developments take place to improve radio communication. Radar becomes a reality, and the invention of the magnetron makes microwave links possible.

1945 Arthur C Clarke put forward the idea of communication satellites.

1947 The first semiconductor switch, the transistor is invented.

1954 Colour television broadcasts begin in the USA.

1956 The first transatlantic telephone cable TAT-1 opened, giving 36 telephone circuits.

1957 The USSR launched Sputnik, the first satellite and started the Space Age.

1958 In the UK it becomes possible to dial long distance telephone calls, without being connected by an operator.

1959 The invention of the integrated circuit, which is made up of many transistors on a small piece of silicon about 0·5 cm^2.

1962 Telstar launched and live television pictures from America received in the UK.

Left: Claude Chappe invented his optical telegraph in 1790. At this time France was in turmoil and in desperate need of a quick and reliable communications system. It was used purely for military purposes and was both expensive to build and to run.

1963 It becomes possible to dial directly from London to Paris.

1965 Early Bird, the first commercial geostationary satellite, launched into orbit by INTELSAT.

1966 Optical fibre communication suggested by Kao and Hockham.

1974 Oscar 7 launched for amateur radio operators to communicate by satellite.

1977 The world's first optical fibre link established between Hitchin and Stevenage in the UK, carrying about 2,000 telephone circuits.

1979 Intelsat V launched into orbit with a capacity of 12,000 circuits.

1980 Cable television systems begin to be commercially used in USA and UK.

1981 Voyagers 1 and 2 launched to explore the solar system.

Books to read

Telecommunications by M.J. Barnes, published by Wayland.

Science in a topic: Communication by D. Kincaid and P.S. Coles, published by Hulton.

How it works: The Telephone by D. Carey, published by Ladybird.

How it works: The Television by D. Carey, published by Ladybird.

Telecommunications – a technology for change by E. Davies, published by HMSO.

Understanding Telecommunications by M. Overman, published by Lutterworth Press.

The World Communicates by M. Rickards, published by Longmans.

The Communications Revolution by E. Wrangham, published by Harrap.

John Logie Baird and Television by M. Hallett, published by Wayland.

Acknowledgements

Photographs
Aldus Archive: 6; 7; 8B; 10T; 14BR; 46
BBC Hulton Picture Library: 8T; 27
Paul Brierly: Contents page
British Telecom Photo Library: 13; 31; 33B; 38; 39; 40; 41
British Telecom Technology Showcase: 14BL; 17 T & BL
Bundesministeriums für das Post- und Fernmeldewesen, Bonn: 17BR
Ferranti Electronics Ltd.: 37
GEC Marconi Ltd.: 20
Michael Holford: 10B; 22BR
Imperial War Museum/Aldus Archive: 25
Mansell Collection: 47
Ministère des PTT, Paris: 29; 30
NASA: 35T
Science Museum: 22BL; 26
Space Frontiers: 35B
ZEFA: Cover

Key: T(top); B(bottom); L(left); R(right).

Artists
Michael Robinson
Julia Osorno

Left: James Clerk Maxwell, a professor of mathematics, predicted the existence of radio waves in 1864. His claims were rejected however and his work did not achieve recognition until after his death.

Index